ABANDONED MANSIONS OF IRELAND

ABANDONED MANSIONS OF IRELAND

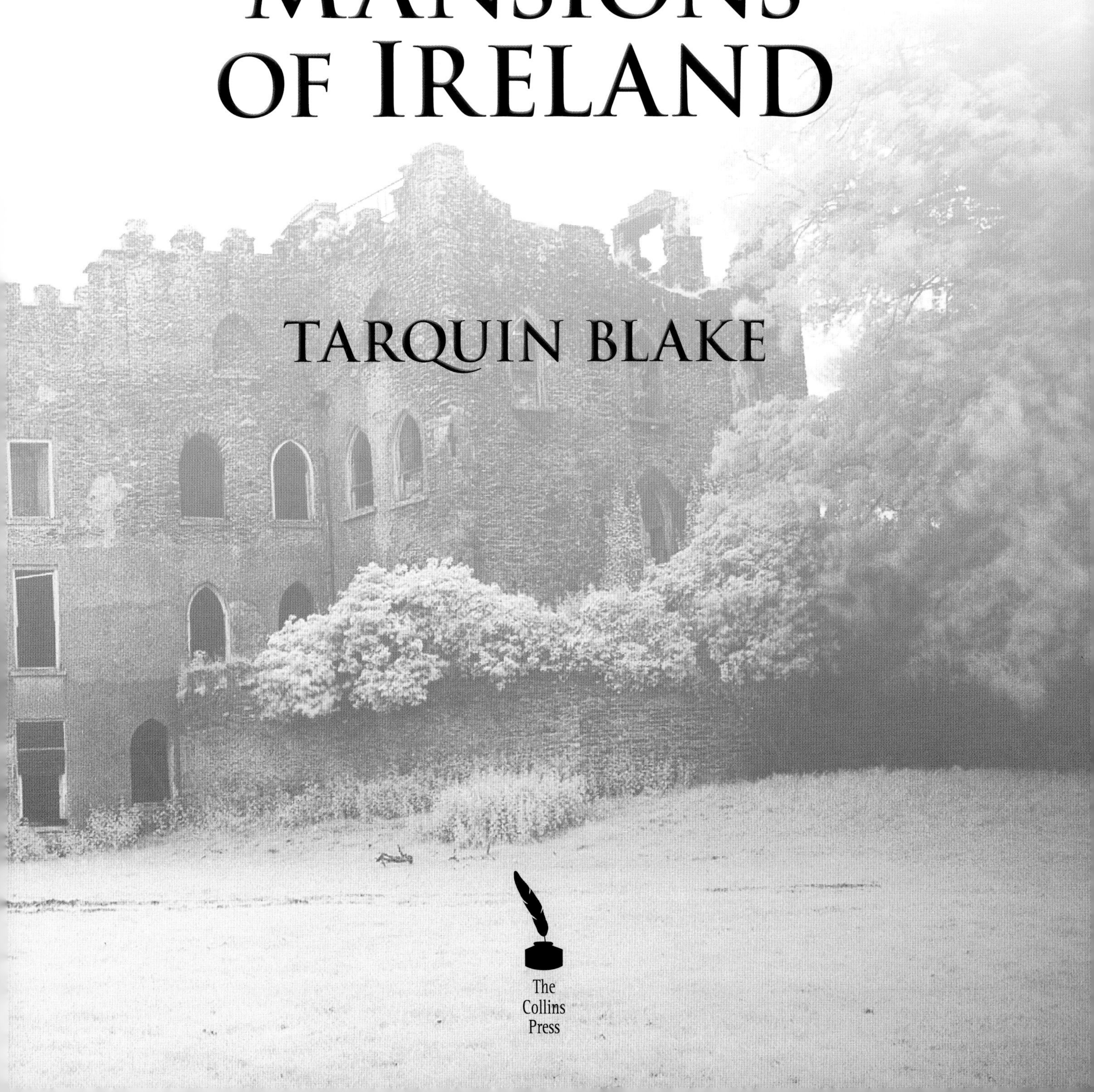

TARQUIN BLAKE

The
Collins
Press

First published in 2010 by
The Collins Press
West Link Park
Doughcloyne
Wilton
Cork

Reprinted 2011, 2012

British Library Cataloguing in Publication Data

Blake, Tarquin.
Abandoned mansions of Ireland.
1. Mansions—Ireland—History—Pictorial works.
2. Abandoned houses—Ireland—History—Pictorial works.
3. Upper class—Dwellings—Ireland—History—Pictorial works.
I. Title
728.8'09415-dc22

ISBN-13: 9781848890619

Design and typesetting by Fairways Design

Typeset in Garamond 11.5/13

Printed in Italy by Printer Trento

Photograph on p. vii: steps leading to Coole Park, house demolished 1941.

Contents

To Fiona and Aoibhe, who have long put up with my
obsession with ruined country mansions.
Also to all those who helped me along the way.

'Here, traveller, scholar, poet, take your stand
When all those rooms and passages are gone,
When nettles wave upon a shapeless mound
And saplings root among the broken stone . . .'

~ 'Coole Park, 1929' by William Butler Yeats

Preface

For years I went off exploring the lost and failing architecture of Rome, Greece, Cambodia, Egypt, Mexico and other far corners of this earth. I was blissfully unaware that some of the most amazing things I have ever seen were almost on my own doorstep.

In 2008 I started exploring the lost architecture of Ireland. The things I found astonished and surprised me – how could so much be lost and forgotten; did anybody care? I set up the website www.AbandonedIreland.com to document and publish my discoveries.

The exploration of abandoned country mansion houses became something of an addiction and in the winter of 2008 I buried myself in every available book, manuscript and fading map I could lay my hands on. In 2009 I set out with the intention of visiting and documenting every big house ruin still standing in some shape or form in the Republic of Ireland. I travelled north to south, east to west and then back again. I camped out in plenty of decaying old mansions. I explored hundreds of ruins. Some people find history and heritage boring, but in my efforts to track down and photograph these ruins I have had the most astonishing adventures.

The locations I have selected to include in this book are a diverse mix. I started by trying to include a couple of locations from each county, then houses with varied degrees of disintegration: some still have roofs, others are little more than a pile of rubble. I have also included a few castles and a mill. Castleboro in County Wexford and Dromore in County Limerick must rate among the most remarkable ruins in the whole of Ireland, while others like Kincraigie in County Cork would be almost unheard of.

I will end this note with a plea for lost heritage: the abandoned mansions of Ireland are slowly disintegrating, and memory of them fading. It is up to us to make sure they are not completely forgotten. If you would like to share facts, folklore or old photographs then I can be contacted through my website www.AbandonedIreland.com which is continuously updated with mansions, asylums, forts, relics of industry, convents and castles.

Tarquin Blake

Disclaimer

Readers should note that this is an information guide and does not act as an invitation to enter any of the properties or sites listed. Most of the properties listed are in private hands and permission would be required from the owner before visiting. Ruins are hazardous. No responsibility is accepted by the author or publisher for any loss, injury or inconvenience sustained by anyone as a result of using this book.

Introduction

From the middle of the eighteenth century the Irish country house flourished. Land was owned by a relatively small number of large landowners. Through plantation and conquest by England, the majority of landowners were the Anglo-Irish, Protestant ascendancy. Land was worked by tenant farmers who paid rent to the landowning elite.

The landowners could easily afford a comfortable life. At the end of the eighteenth century, Arthur Young, an English agriculturist, recorded in his journal that an Irish gentleman could comfortably keep a carriage, four horses, three menservants, three maids and a nurse for about £500 a year. In these times the wage of a footman or a good cook was only six guineas a year, a housemaid might cost £3, a kitchen maid £2 and a butler's wage might run to £12. For example, Baron Louth, residing at Louth Hall, had a modest estate of around 3,000 acres from which, in 1830, he received £4,499, equating to nearly 400 times the wage of his butler, or nearly 700 times the wage of his cook. With this comfortable income, the Baron had a fine existence and could afford to extend Louth Hall with a vast three-storey wing in 1760 and then in 1805 to remodel the entire structure.

By 1850 however, the Great Famine had taken its toll. Starving, penniless tenants could not pay rent and soon many country estates found their finances seriously in decline. In 1849 the Encumbered Estates Court was set up to undertake the sale of bankrupted estates and from 1850 to 1858 some 8,000 estates changed hands.

The land ownership reforms of the late 1800s removed much of the landlords' control over their tenants. After the 1881 Land Act, rents fixed by the land court began to reduce the landlords' income. The Ashbourne Act of 1885 introduced the system of state-aided land purchase, and then, in 1903 the Wyndham Land Purchase Act saw around three-quarters of tenants buying out their landlord. Some 9 million acres were transferred directly into the hands of the farmers. The estate houses, stripped of their land and with little other means to raise income, soon fell into decline.

From 1919 to 1923, during the War of Independence and the Irish Civil War, the country house became a target for the Irish Republican Army. Sometimes their Anglo-Irish occupiers were sympathetic to the British government and in other cases the large houses could be used to billet troops; for both these reasons houses were deliberately burnt. For the remainder of the twentieth century the ever increasing expense of maintaining these large mansion houses made them unviable.

Many houses were abandoned and soon forgotten, hundreds were simply demolished, and others lay forgotten at the back of farmers' fields or were slowly swallowed by forest.

County Carlow
Clogrenan House

Clogrenan House, home of the Rochforts, was built early in the nineteenth century. The three-storey, five-bay, neo-classical country house is attributed to the architect Thomas Cobden who also designed Carlow Cathedral and Duckett's Grove House.

The remains of the early sixteenth-century Clogrenan Castle, which had been home to the Dukes of Ormonde, was transformed into an entranceway to the new Clogrenan Estate.

J. N. Brewer, writing after his visit to Clogrenan in 1815, described the location as 'abounding in natural charms, and further enriched by some noble vestiges of antiquity'. He described the house itself as 'of modern erection and a plain building, respectable in character and extremely commodious'.

360° view of house interior from basement level

The Rochfort family was established in County Carlow from the early eighteenth century. John Rochfort was High Sheriff of County Carlow in 1758; his son and heir, Colonel John Staunton Rochfort, was also High Sheriff in 1823.

In 1819 workmen discovered a hoard of archaeological objects at the ford of the River Barrow, a short distance from Clogrenan; brazen swords, arrowheads, a skull and other human bones. It was reported that Colonel John Staunton Rochfort regretted that the workmen who discovered these antiquities had 'privately disposed of nearly the whole lot' before he became aware of their find.

The remains of the sixteenth-century Clogrenan Castle are a National Monument

Colonel John Staunton Rochfort's son and heir, Colonel Horace William Noel Rochfort, born in 1809, was Deputy Lord Lieutenant, Justice of the Peace and High Sheriff of County Carlow in 1840. He was a sportsman and athlete of some distinction; he founded the Carlow Cricket Club in 1831, the Carlow Rugby Club (now known as the Carlow Football Club) and also the All Ireland Polo Club in 1873. The All Ireland Polo Club is the longest-established polo club in Europe.

View to remains of cantilevered stone dog-leg staircase

Front hall with view to side corridor

The 1911 census records Clogrenan as occupied by: Horace Rochfort, aged 33, farmer; Horace's wife Violet Rochfort, aged 34; and their daughter Helene Rochfort, aged 3. The house was staffed by two domestic servants: Jane Kenny, aged 60, and Mary Walsh, aged 20.

In 1922 Horace Rochfort sold the Clogrenan estate to the Waterford builder John Heron, who cut down most of the estate's woodland. Clogrenan House was still habitable in 1935. The property changed hands once again and by 1945 the roof had been removed and the house abandoned.

Basement corridor

Front hall interior looking through front door

View of front entrance

County Carlow
Holloden House

View of house from northwest

Holloden House, originally called Malcolm Ville, was built for a Mr Mulhallen around 1760. The house is two storeys over basement and joined on one side by a curved curtain wall leading to an octagonal pavilion. Holloden House subsequently became home to Colonel Philip Doyne Vigors.

The Vigors family of Carlow can be traced back to Rev. Louis Vigors of Holloden, Devon, England. Rev. Louis Vigors first appears in records in Ireland as the Vicar of Kilfaughnabeg, County Cork, in the year 1615.

By 1781 Rev. Edward Vigors, the Rector of Shankill, was residing a short distance from Malcolm Ville at Burgage House, County Carlow. Rev. Edward Vigors' son and heir, Rev. Thomas Mercer Vigors, who was ordained on 26 March 1797, was the Rector of Powerstown. His son Philip Doyne Vigors did not follow his father into the Church and instead chose a military career, serving in the 11th and 19th Regiments in Australia, Burma and India. He was promoted to Major on 7 March 1870 and Lieutenant-Colonel on 1 October 1877. He commanded the 1st Battalion 19th Foot from 15 March 1879 until he retired on full pay with the honorary rank of Colonel on 12 January 1881.

Colonel Philip Doyne Vigors acquired Malcolm Ville and renamed it Holloden House after his ancestors' home in Devon, England. He became Vice-President of the Royal Society of Antiquaries of Ireland and published numerous articles in the society journals.

On the Colonel's death in 1903, his wife, Margaret Vigors, became the head of the house.

The 1911 census records the occupants of Holloden as Margaret Vigors, aged 58, and her daughter Esther Vigors, aged 26. The house had a staff of three: Julia Purcell, aged 46, cook; Annie Doyle, aged 22, parlour maid; and Sarah Cane, aged 19, maid.

Holloden House was inherited by Esther Alice Vigors. She married Major Standish de Courcy O'Grady. Esther died aged 86 on 24 July 1970; her daughter Faith O'Grady resided at Holloden until at least 1976.

Holloden House now stands silent, slowly becoming encased in the undergrowth.

Internal view of outbuildings

View into yard at side of house

Cloverhill House

In 1799 James Sanderson employed the architect Francis Johnston to build Cloverhill House. Johnston also designed Ballynagall House (see p. 304) but is best known for designing Nelson's Pillar and the General Post Office on O'Connell Street, Dublin. (The Post Office was rebuilt after being partly destroyed in the 1916 Easter Rising and still survives in fine condition today. The Pillar, however, was blown up by a group of former IRA men in 1966, during 'Operation Humpty Dumpty'.)

By 1804 Cloverhill House was complete. The house was three storeys over basement (visible on the side elevation), with the top storey concealed on the three-bay front entrance side.

360° view of basement

In 1837 Cloverhill was described in Lewis' *Topographical Dictionary* as 'an excellent mansion, the seat of J. Sanderson, Esq., has also a very beautiful demesne, richly adorned, and bordered by a spacious lake'.

The Cloverhill demesne was inherited by James Sanderson's daughter Lucy, who married Samuel Winter in 1826. Lucy passed Cloverhill to her third son, Samuel Winter, with the provision that he take the name Sanderson. In 1873 Samuel took both the surname and arms of Sanderson by Royal Licence.

The entrance to the Cloverhill estate is by a magnificent gate

The 1911 census records the occupants of Cloverhill as Samuel Sanderson, aged 76, retired farmer, and his wife Ann Sanderson, aged 73. The Sandersons had a staff of seven: Mary Trenier, aged 71, cook; Alice Kingston, aged 50, maid; Sara Lilburn, aged 29, maid; Harriett Dundas, aged 34, maid; Ann Weldon, aged 57, laundress; Annie Clarke, aged 30, kitchen maid; and John Kemp, aged 22, groom.

Interior ground floor looking upwards

View of basement, staircase to upper levels through arch centre left of photograph

Back staircase

When Samuel Sanderson died without children, Cloverhill was inherited by his nephew, John James Purdon. Purdon died unmarried in 1933, leaving his nephew, Major John Nugent Purdon, to inherit Cloverhill. The Major sold Cloverhill around 1958.

The Sanderson family motto is *Toujours propice*, which translates as 'Always propitious'.

◀ View of windows in side elevation

▼ Cloverhill front door

View from front entrance hall to rear of house

Lisnagowan House

Around 1820 Lisnagowan House was built as a dower house for the Humphrys family of Ballyhaise House. Mrs Humphrys is recorded as occupying Lisnagowan by Lewis in his *Topographical Dictionary* of 1837.

The house takes its name from the townland in which it is located, the name of which originates from Irish and means the fort of O'Gowan. The Lisnagowan ring fort lies a short distance from Lisnagowan House.

View from the southwest

Lisnagowan House remained in the hands of the Humphrys, and was occupied by Armitage Eglantine Humphrys. It was later rented to a Mr Weir by the landlord, Nugent Winter Humphrys, as recorded in the census of 1911.

Ballyhaise House was sold by Nugent Winter Humphrys, and is now an agricultural college. Lisnagowan House, long ago abandoned, stands as a lonely ruin.

The Humphrys family motto, *Optima Speranda Spira*, translates as 'Hoping for the best, I live'.

View from basement level up to
drawing-room window on ground floor

Staircase window

Small outbuilding adjoining house and stable yard

Rear entrance into house basement

County Clare
Clooney House

D avid Bindon, MP for Ennis, acquired the Clooney estate around 1670. The Bindon family owned a considerable amount of land in Counties Clare and Limerick. Francis Bindon was born at Clooney in 1698 and in 1723 under a settlement with his father was assigned the family estate. Francis studied at the Academy of Painting and Drawing in London and became a member of the Royal Dublin Society. He became a successful portrait painter and, since he was a wealthy gentleman with good connections, attracted many notable patrons including Jonathan Swift. Francis painted successfully for several years

360° view of house interior (staircase in centre of photograph)

but around 1733 he began to study architecture in the Office of the Surveyor General, Sir Edward Lovatt Pearce. He went on to design many large country houses, including Carnelly and Newhall in County Clare, and Bessborough, Woodstock and Castle Morres in County Kilkenny. He worked with the Palladian architect Richard Castle on the design of Russborough House, County Wicklow, completing it after Castle died in 1751. The west wing of Russborough House was gutted by fire on 7 February 2010. Francis also designed St John's Square in Limerick.

View of front entrance

It is believed that Clooney House was redesigned by Francis prior to his death in 1765. He died 'suddenly in his chariot on his way to the country' and the same obituary notice in *Faulkner's Journal* described him as 'one of the best painters and architects this nation ever produced. He was a most polite well-bred gentleman and an excellent scholar, which he improved with his travels abroad.'

Francis' brother Nicholas was then granted the lands of Clooney and continued to live at the house until his death, when the Clooney estate was left to his nephew, Burton Bindon of Limerick.

In 1855 Clooney House was unoccupied, with the lands of 195 acres farmed by Mr Thomas Spaight. Burton Bindon, experiencing financial difficulties, sold the house through the Encumbered Estates Court to Henry White for £8,075 and then emigrated to Australia with his daughter.

A few years later Miss Bindon married Joseph Hall. They returned to Ireland in 1859, and purchased the now burnt-out shell of the house. They rebuilt the house and re-established the estate as a farm which consisted of 604 acres.

Mr Hall had come to Ireland with the small fortune of £9,000 but died in 1907 without leaving enough money for his own burial. It is said he was a gambler and his wife extravagant. On 25 March 1909 Mrs Hall, who at that time refused to sell any of the lands, was under the police protection of a sergeant and three constables. However, later that year the lands were bought out by the tenants under the Wyndham Land Act purchase scheme.

Side view of house

View from basement level

Ivy-covered console
bracket on doorway

The chimney stack now lies in the basement

View from house to rear outbuildings

The 1911 census shows Ellen Hall, aged 76, residing at Clooney House with Lizzy Loughton, aged 71, and their servant Kate White, aged 23.

In 1924 Clooney House was destroyed in an accidental fire and in 1928 the Clooney estate, consisting of house, land and remaining buildings was bought by Mrs L. D. Tuckey. From 1930 to 1944 Clooney House was occupied by Mr James Doherty who restored some of the buildings, however, in 1944 all buildings were described as ruins and the land had been divided up among local farmers.

Clooney House now stands as an impressive ruin. The archway, which once held a walnut-panelled, fan-lit hall door, is covered by an iron gate to keep out the cattle that graze across the former front lawns.

County Clare
Doonass House

Hugh Massy, a general in Cromwell's army, came to Ireland in 1641. He settled in Duntryleague, County Limerick. His son, also named Hugh, married Amy Benson, the daughter of another Cromwellian general. The last of their four sons, Charles Massy, was ordained around 1720 and became vicar of Abington and Murroe, County Limerick, and in 1740 Dean of St Mary's Cathedral, Limerick. In 1739 a perpetual lease was made of the ancient castle of Doonass by the Earl of Thomond to Charles Massy for £212 per annum.

Charles Massy married Grace Dillon; they had two daughters and one son, Hugh, who took the surname Dillon-Massy. Hugh went on to become MP for Clare in 1766 and 1783 and was created a baronet

360° view of central hallway

in 1781, becoming Sir Hugh Dillon-Massy. During an argument with Sir Lucius O'Brien of Dromoland Castle, Dillon-Massy was challenged to a duel. O'Brien was defeated but both men survived.

Sir Hugh Dillon-Massy had three children: his first son, also named Hugh, born in 1767, became the second baronet on his father's death; Charles, born in 1770, obtained holy orders and became rector of Kiltenanlea and Killokennedy; Mary Frances Massy, born in 1771, drowned while crossing the Shannon in a boat in 1794. According to local lore she had quarrelled with Lord Clare of Mountshannon, which is downstream and on the opposite side of the Shannon to Doonass. In her haste to leave his company she

Abandoned furniture in front room

Upstairs landing

procured a local gillie to row her across the river in a thick fog. Tragedy struck when the boat was swept over some rocks and both Mary and the boatman were drowned.

Sir Hugh Dillon-Massy, first baronet, died in 1807 and was succeeded by his first son Hugh, who also became an MP for Clare between 1798 and 1802. Around 1820 the second baronet remodelled Doonass house with a late Georgian villa style front. This is the only part of Doonass House which remains today. On the death of the second baronet in 1842, the estate and title passed to Hugh's nephew, also named Hugh. This Hugh was a magistrate and Deputy Lieutenant for County Clare, appointed High Sheriff in 1833 and was also a captain in the Limerick militia.

The famine of the 1840s took its toll on the Doonass estate: no rents were sought or paid and the Massy family contributed generously to various famine relief efforts. Eventually the estate was almost bankrupt. In 1858 the Broadford part of the estate was sold in the Encumbered Estates Court, allowing the remaining debts to be paid off.

Sir Hugh, third baronet, died in Dun Laoghaire, County Dublin, in 1870. He had no male heir and so the baronetcy died with him. His tenants erected a large monument in his memory engraved with the following:

ERECTED BY THE GRATEFUL TENANTRY TO THE MEMORY OF THE GOOD SIR HUGH DILLON-MASSY BARONET OF DOONASS HOUSE WHO DEPARTED THIS LIFE ON 29TH OCTOBER 1870 AGED 70 YEARS

This monument stood at the crossroads in Clonlara village until it was demolished in 1956.

When Hugh's wife, Lady Mary Dillon-Massy died in 1890, her nephew John Westropp of Attyflin inherited the estate. The will stipulated that he assume the name Massy. He thus became John Massy-Westropp. He was succeeded by his son, Colonel John Massy-Westropp.

In 1910 the estate was sold to the tenants under the Land Acts. From the original 4,625 acres, all that remained was what lay inside the demesne walls.

The 1911 census records the occupants as: John Massy-Westropp, aged 50, retired colonel; his wife Georgina Massy-Westropp, aged 43; and son John Francis Ralph Massy-Westropp, aged 19. The Massy-Westropps had two servants: Mary Morgan, aged 30 and Lee Kate, aged 23.

Colonel John Massy-Westropp was spoiled for choice when it came to impressive residences. Through inheritance, he had acquired Doonass House, Attyflin and Bunratty Castle. He sold Doonass and Attyflin and died at Bunratty in 1943.

Upstairs bedroom

Debris-filled kitchen (it appears to be a corridor that was converted into a kitchen in later years).

View of hallway after the fire
(no trace of the fine staircase remains)

Doonass House after it was destroyed by fire in 2009

During the construction of the dam at Ardnacrusha, part of the Shannon Hydro-Electric Scheme, a group of eighteen German engineers, scientists, and electricians lived in Doonass House. On 12 June 1926 they received a summons from the local gardaí as 1,400 bottles of German wine valued at £700 pounds had been seized. There were two cellars at the house, one for the residents and one for German callers. Ernest Fiege, the mess steward at the house, was fined £10 for selling liquor without a licence.

During the Emergency, as the Second World War is often called in Ireland, Doonass was requisitioned by the Department of Defence and used to billet troops. In the 1940s and 1950s Lady O'Brien rented the house. The Buckley family, proprietors of the *Limerick Leader,* briefly owned it and the Sheehy family rented it for a number of years before buying nearby Belle Isle House.

View of outbuildings behind house

Benjamin Weizmann bought the Doonass estate in the late 1950s. He was the eldest son of Chaim Weizmann, biochemist, Zionist and first president of Israel in 1948. Benjamin Weizmann was considered to be a colourful and generous character. He demolished the older back wing of the house, and restored the Regency front.

Some years later Mr Weizmann sold Doonass House for £20,000. Dr Leahy owned the house for a while, before selling it to Ms Marie O'Sullivan for £19,000. The house was occupied by Ms O'Sullivan and Mrs Griffin until around 1999.

In 2009 a group of teenagers broke into the house and started a fire in one of the bedrooms. The fire was fanned by the breeze through an open window and quickly spread out of control to the rest of the house. Despite the efforts of five fire engines the house was completely gutted.

Buttevant Castle

The town of Buttevant derives its name from the war cry *Boutez en avant* ('push forward') of David de Barry as he drove his men on against the McCarthys. That phrase went on to be used as the family motto of the Viscounts Buttevant.

Built around the year 1200, the Castle of Buttevant, seated boldly on an outcrop of rock above the River Awbeg, had become the main residence of the Clan of Donegan. The Clan refused to surrender the castle to the English, and rejected every attempt to take the castle by force. Eventually the Donegan garrison was surprised and captured by David de Barry. It is said de Barry gained it through the corruption

360° view of castle interior

and treachery of a soldier in the castle garrison. After taking the castle and slaughtering its sleeping inmates, de Barry rewarded the betraying soldier with the removal of his head. According to legend the gruesome severed head was cast down the stairs of one of the castle towers, still yelling one word 'Treachery! Treachery! Treachery!'. The headless soldier is said to haunt the castle today.

On 24 February 1206, King John of England confirmed de Barry with the lordships of Castlelyons, Buttevant and Barry's Court in East Cork. The family would eventually acquire the honours of Viscount Buttevant and Earl of Barrymore.

The front entrance appears to reuse medieval stonework (perhaps from a nearby abbey)

In 1568 the castle was taken by the Lord Deputy Sir Henry Sydney but was then regained by the de Barrys and held until the early nineteenth century when it was sold to Sir John Anderson, founder of the town of Fermoy. Sir John rebuilt and extended the castle, transforming it into a comfortable mansion house.

In 1812, during the planting of the castle grounds, a human skeleton was discovered. The skull was reported to have a wild growth of hair which instantly disintegrated when exposed to air. Around the body was concealed a stash of old coins.

Sir John Anderson and his son James Caleb Anderson went on to build a mill adjoining Buttevant Castle (see p. 54). When Sir John Anderson died, James Caleb Anderson inherited his father's title and the castle. Unfortunately the Andersons' finances had suffered through their construction projects and Sir James sold the castle to the Viscount Doneraile.

Arched window on to fortifications

A series of broken passageways lead up into the castle interior

View of small turret above the castle walls

In 1854 George W. Whitelocke-Lloyd of Strancally Castle, County Waterford, purchased the castle but because his wife was not keen on the residence it was let to various tenants. The Browning family occupied the house and worked the adjoining mill until 1865. The Rev. W. H. Cotter occupied the castle until 1893. William Guinea resided there until 1901 when the castle estate was purchased by Matthew Nagle. The roof was then removed and Buttevant Castle dismantled.

ANDERSON.

County Cork

Buttevant Mill

Buttevant Mill was built by Sir John Anderson and his son James early in the nineteenth century. In its time it was among the largest and most modern mills in the county. Reflecting the design of the adjoining Buttevant Castle, the Andersons added battlements to the top of the mill.

James Anderson began working with steam power at the mill and went on to develop several patents: in 1837, for improvements in locomotive engines, and in 1846, for improvements in obtaining motive power and applying it to the propulsion of cars and vessels and the driving of machinery. For his 1831 patent, he produced a carriage in which twenty-four men were arranged seated in two rows, one above the other. By an

360° view of mill top floor interior

arrangement of gears the men drove the carriage by a rowing motion and a fair speed could be reached.

In the *Mechanic's Magazine* of June 1839, a Dublin reporter wrote 'I was fortunate enough to get a sight of Sir James Anderson's steam carriage, with which I was much pleased. It had just arrived from the country, and was destined for London in about three weeks. The engine weighs ten tons, and will, I dare say, act very well. I shall have an opportunity of judging that, as the tender is at Cork. It has a sort of diligence, not joined, but to be attached to the tender, making in all three carriages. I talked a great deal about it to one of his principal men, who was most lavish in its praises, especially as regards the boiler.'

A worker's forgotten shoe sits next to long-idle machinery

Anderson went on to develop steam carriages which were tested on the Howth Road, Dublin. He had plans that all the main towns in Ireland would be connected by the operation of his steam carriages; these plans, however, did not come to fruition and Anderson received little financial reward for devoting thirty years of his life to the development of steam carriages on Irish roads.

By 1837 Lewis reported in his *Topographical Dictionary* that the Buttevant Mill, while capable of producing 20,000 barrels of flour a year, was not in operation.

The mill later became the property of Thomas Walsh of Mallow. Anderson also sold his adjoining residence, Buttevant Castle, to Viscount Doneraile.

Sir James Anderson died in London on 4 April 1886, aged 69, and, as he had no male descendant, his title died out with him.

The Browning family worked Buttevant Mill until 1865. William Richardson Oliver was the proprietor until 1918. The mill was badly damaged by fire in 1932. In 1967 Furney McCay & Co Ltd were in operation, and in 1976 the Greens of Cork took over. Dairygold Co-Operative Society Ltd finally bought out Buttevant Mill in 1993.

Buttevant Mill now lies silent, the roof leaks and the floorboards slowly rot and crumble.

▲ Window & wheel

▼ The text on the old sack reads 'Furney McCay & Co Ltd, Buttevant, 1967'

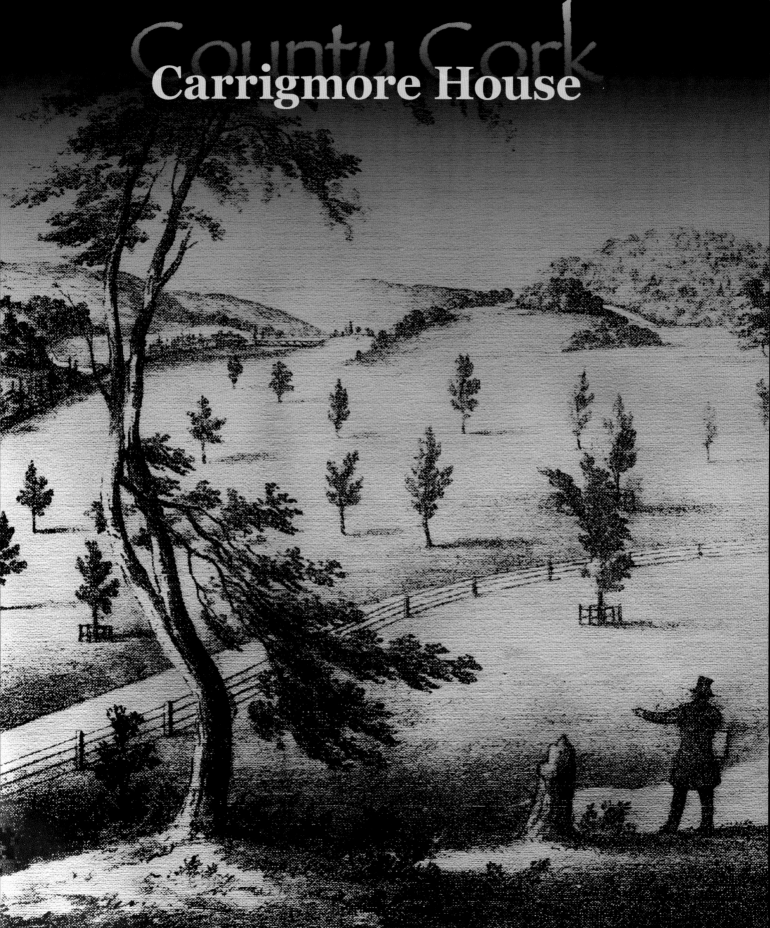

Carrigmore House was originally called Connorville, home of the O'Connors. It is said that Mr O'Connor was slain by Cromwell's soldiers and that his widow fled to Bandon, carrying her young child, Cornelius, and a contingency of gold coins sewn into her coat. Over time the O'Connors became successful merchants and purchased various lands around County Cork. The 'O' was dropped in favour of the English-sounding name, Conner.

In 1721 William Conner married Anne, daughter of Roger Bernard of Palace Anne who was a brother of Judge Bernard of Castle Bernard. In 1727 William Conner built Connorville House, and planted the demesne

Part of the staircase still clings to the wall

William's son and heir, Roger Conner, married Anne Longfield, sister of Richard, Viscount Longueville. Roger Conner had five sons; his three older sons, Daniel, William and Robert, kept the name Conner but his two younger sons, Roger and Arthur, reverted their name to O'Connor.

Robert Conner went on to build himself a mansion, Fort Robert, a short distance from Connorville (see p. 68).

On the death of his father, Roger O'Connor resided at Connorville. His hatred of British domination extended itself to the tax collector. During the days of the dog tax, when the collector of taxes called

From basement looking upwards. Bath and doors are suspended from collapsed floors

View from basement showing collapsed internal structure

one day for his payment, he enquired, 'Have you got no dogs?' Roger O'Connor replied, 'Not one.' Just at this moment his favourite dog came running into the courtyard. Roger, in an attempt to avoid detection, exclaimed, 'A mad dog, a mad dog!' and both Roger and the terrified tax collector took refuge in the house. No dog tax was paid that day.

When Napoleon Bonaparte was said to be considering the invasion of Ireland, Roger decided that he would entertain the emperor if he did indeed invade. He thought Connorville unworthy of this dignity and moved to Dangan Castle, County Meath (see p. 252). At that time Dangan Castle was described as a most magnificent residence, but under the care of Roger O'Connor, Dangan was burnt down and the once finely wooded demesne transformed into a shabby wreck. In a strange quirk of fate, Dangan Castle was the birthplace of Arthur Wellesley, Duke of Wellington, who defeated Napoleon Bonaparte at the Battle of Waterloo on Sunday 18 June 1815.

In 1842 James Lysaght purchased the Connorville estate. He rebuilt the house at a cost exceeding £4,000, renaming it Carrigmore House. However, the Famine years took their toll and it was only seventeen years later that the bankrupted estate was put up for auction in the Encumbered Estate sales.

The 1859 Encumbered Estate auction catalogue lists Carrigmore as a highly valuable estate in first-rate order. As listed on the auction particulars, the estate comprised farming lands, a fox cover, woods which offered early and superior woodcock shooting and also excellent snipe and partridge shooting. The gardens surrounding the house were described as being laid out in excellent taste and planted with a variety of exotic and indigenous evergreens and flowering shrubs and trees. The residence was described as containing on the first floor a well-proportioned hall and vestibule, an easy staircase, a drawing room 21½ feet by 18 feet, a dining room 21½ feet by 18 feet, a library 18 feet by 13 feet, a breakfast room 18 feet by 12 feet, a store room and a water closet. The second floor contained five bedchambers, a dressing room, bathroom and another water closet. The outbuildings included domestic offices and agricultural buildings, a gardener's lodge and a laundry. Carrigmore was, however, withdrawn from auction and sold privately to James L. Homes.

During the following decades, Carrigmore changed hands several times; in 1879 it was sold to James Purcell, to Henry Connor in 1893 and to James Morton in 1905.

The 1911 census records the occupants as: James Henry Morton, aged 52, gentleman; his wife Emily Mary Morton, aged 57; and his mother Mary Katherine Morton, aged 92. The Mortons had a staff of six: Elizabeth Francis McDonnell, aged 43, nurse and companion; Joseph Albert Kerr, aged 30, steward; Mary Mahony, aged 23, parlour maid; Catherine Connelly, aged 20, housemaid; Mary Ann Hourihan, aged 25, cook; and Bridget Hourihan, aged 20, dairy maid.

Carrigmore was sold to Andrew Kellaher in 1924. Andrew Kellaher junior was still in residence in 1933. The last person to live at Carrigmore was Mrs R. Langran.

Carbery Milk Products purchased sections of the Carrigmore estate in 1965. Dubliner Cheese is now made in the adjoining factory.

View from basement showing collapsed beams

View of front entrance (the house is now surrounded by undergrowth)

County Cork
Fort Robert

Fort Robert, a weather-slated, eight-bay house of two storeys over basement, was built by Robert Conner in 1788. Robert Conner's father, Roger Conner resided at Connorville House (Connorville was later renamed Carrigmore House, see p. 61).

Robert Conner, although not in the army, had military notions. He formed his own corps (which, it is said, he pronounced *corpse*) of local volunteer fighters. Robert had such an exaggerated opinion of his impressive corps that he scared his wife by threatening to invade France and bring back Napoleon in an iron cage to suspend in the hall of Fort Robert. Robert was in continuous communication with the authorities at Dublin Castle. One letter he sent was addressed 'My dear Government'. When an acquaintance of his, Sir Francis

View of front room from basement

Burdett, was asked to comment on another of Robert's manuscripts, Sir Francis replied that he was no judge of music. Robert's clumsy manuscript contained so many blotches with sentences underscored by numerous lines that to Sir Francis' eye it resembled some kind of comical musical notation.

Robert died around 1820 and it is said his ghost still haunts Carrigmore Wood, where at midnight it careers at lightning speed at the head of a spectral hunt with many bloodcurdling shrieks and yells. Robert's son, Arthur O'Connor, became the new head of the Fort Robert household. Arthur O'Connor died in 1828 leaving his son Feargus O'Connor to inherit the Fort Robert house and demesne.

71

View from front entrance

Feargus O'Connor studied law at Trinity College, Dublin, and was called to the Irish Bar. He became a lawyer but then entered parliament as an MP for County Cork in 1832. Three years later he was expelled for failing to meet the property qualification for MPs.

In 1837 he emerged in England, establishing a weekly radical newspaper, *The Northern Star*, and went on to become a leader and one of the most popular speakers of the Chartist Movement, a movement for political and social reform which took its name from the People's Charter of 1838.

Internal view looking upwards

By 1848, it was becoming obvious that Feargus had a troubled mind. Finally in 1852 he is said to have caused great insult in the House of Commons, as a result of which he was taken into the custody of the sergeant at arms. The next day he was pronounced insane and committed to Dr Tuke's asylum at Chiswick.

Meanwhile back at Fort Robert, the mansion house was falling into ruin. By 1854 it was empty and decayed. When Feargus O'Connor died in 1855, it was said that 50,000 people attended his funeral.

Fort Robert was in total ruin by the end of nineteenth century.

County Cork
Kincraigie

In the nineteenth century Kincraigie House was the home of William Burton Leslie, Justice of the Peace for Courtmacsherry. At this time the town was a popular spot for sea bathing and during the summer season it was occupied mainly by visitors. Leslie opened his magnificent flower garden and grounds to visitors on Tuesdays and Thursdays.

The name Kincraigie originates from Leslie's ancestor, Patrick Leslie, fifth Laird of Kincraigie, Scotland. Three generations later the Leslies had crossed the Irish Sea and founded another branch of the family. Rev. Patrick Leslie was the Rector of Monaghan in 1661 and his son, Rev. John Leslie, Rector of Kilmacrenan, purchased the manor and castle of Kincraigie, County Donegal, in 1679. A descendant, John

360° view of house interior

Leslie of Cork, born in 1766, become agent to the third Earl of Shannon, and resided on the Earl's estate at Courtmacsherry. John Leslie's son, William Burton Leslie, became agent to the fifth Earl of Shannon, the Hon. Colonel Henry Bentinck Boyle.

William Burton Leslie married Jane Florence MacCartie in 1845. Jane had previously been married to Rev. Horatio Townsend and had a son, Horace, from that marriage. Her first husband had died from fever just seven months after the birth of Horace. Eight-year-old Horace then lived at Kincraigie with his mother and her second husband, until he purchased his commission as an ensign in the 99th Regiment of Foot on 24 November 1857. His regiment was at first stationed in Ireland, then in 1858 it was ordered to

View of rear of house

Aldershot and from there went on a tour of duty to India in 1859. Horace was promoted to Lieutenant in July 1859. In 1860 the 99th Regiment was ordered to China to join the forces fighting in the Second Opium War. During this campaign Horace took part in the suppression of the Taiping Rebellion and the sacking of the Summer Palace in Peking (now Beijing). Horace became a captain in March 1863.

Tradition maintains that as a souvenir of his adventures in Peking, Horace brought back with him a Pekinese dog which allegedly had belonged to the Chinese empress. He presented the dog to his mother and it lived out its days at Kincraigie.

Captain Horace went on to compose two collections of poems and wrote under the pseudonym of 'Induna' for *Field* and *Irish Sportsman* magazines. He continued to reside at Kincraigie until his death in 1904.

View of front entrance

Window with roller blind still in position

The next resident of Kincraigie was Colonel Henry Fane Travers. The colonel's daughter Eleanor married Francis Valentine Johnson. Francis assumed the name Travers and was resident at Kincraigie for some years after. Francis was employed by Clonakilty Urban and Rural District Councils as an engineer and worked on various projects including the Clonakilty Union Workhouse and the Courtmacsherry water supply. He died in Sussex, England, on 6 December 1940, aged 80.

The Earl of Shannon's Courtmacsherry estate was broken up in the 1920s. Today, the flower gardens are long gone and the ruin of Kincraigie House slowly dissolves into the woodland that surrounds it.

Ground floor bay window

County Dublin
Mountpelier Lodge

Mountpelier Lodge, more commonly known as the Dublin Hellfire Club, was built by William Conolly in 1725. Conolly, a speaker in the Irish House of Commons, lawyer and landowner, was one of the wealthiest men in Ireland at that time. His main residence, Castletown House in Celbridge, County Kildare, was the first winged Palladian house in Ireland.

Mountpelier was built as a hunting lodge, situated at 1,275 feet near the summit of Mount Pelier. During its construction, Conolly purportedly destroyed a Neolithic passage tomb which previously existed on the site. Shortly after completion the slated roof of the lodge was blown off in a great storm. Locals

360° view of first floor room

attributed this misfortune to the pagan gods taking revenge for the destruction of the Neolithic tomb. Conolly replaced the roof with an arch of solid stone.

On ground level, the lodge had a large kitchen, servants' quarters and other small rooms. A flight of steps led up to two large rooms and a hall. All windows faced north, giving a magnificent view of Dublin.

After Conolly's death in 1729, the hunting lodge remained unoccupied for a number of years. In May 1735, Richard Parsons, first Earl of Rosse, James Worsdale and Colonel Jack St Leger founded the Dublin Hellfire Club. The club met at the Eagle Tavern on Cork Hill, but the club motto 'Do as you will' was

Front view of Mountpelier Lodge

more vigorously pursued when they met at Mountpelier Lodge. One account tells of various members of the club, who called themselves 'bucks', seated around a large cauldron of steaming *scaltheen*, a potent drink made from whiskey and butter. The group toasted Satan and called for damnation of the Church. A cup of the hot *scaltheen* was then poured over a black cat and its fur set alight. The apparition of a screaming, flaming cat is still reported in the vicinity of Mount Pelier today.

Local tradition tells of a young farmer, who, curious to find out what went on at the club meetings, climbed up to Mount Pelier one night. He was found by the bucks, dragged into the building and forced to witness the night's activities. The next morning he was discovered wandering aimlessly around the area. Tradition says he spent the rest of his life deaf and dumb, unable even to remember his own name.

In 1740 Richard Chappell Whaley presided over the Hellfire Club. One night after various satanic rituals had been performed, the bucks engaged in a drunken orgy. During the revelry a servant spilt whiskey over Whaley. Whaley, a pyromaniac who engaged in setting fire to the thatch of Catholic chapels for sport, threw

View from top of staircase to first floor room   The rooms are covered with green lichen

a cup of brandy over the servant and set him alight. The servant ran screaming, clutching at tapestries which quickly caught fire. Mountpelier Lodge was soon in flames, and many bucks who were too drunk to escape died in the flames. Mountpelier Lodge was destroyed and locals said that God had finally taken His revenge.

Though the Mountpelier meeting place was gone, Richard Chappel Whaley's son Thomas 'Buck' Whaley went on to become the most notorious Hellfire Club member of all. He indulged in bizarre wagers, one time winning £25,000 from the Duke of Leinster by riding to Jerusalem and back within a year. He boasted he had drunk his way around all the holy places. He won a further £12,000 by betting he could ride a stallion through the window of his father's house to the street some 30 feet below. Whaley survived and claimed his prize; the beautiful Arab stallion was, however, killed in the fall.

After seeing a vision of the devil creeping up towards him, Whaley fled Ireland. He died on the Isle of Man, at the age of 34. Sclerosis of the liver finished him off. On his death the Dublin Hellfire Club also ceased to exist.

County Dublin
Westown House

The Bellew family resided at Westown from 1609; the house was then a simple structure. When Peter Hussey married Mary, only daughter and heir of Bartholomew Bellew, the Westown estate became home to the Hussey family. The current Westown House was built in the early eighteenth century.

The Westown estate passed through various members of the Hussey family until Richard Hussey died, leaving the estate to his cousin Gerald Strong. Gerald assumed the name and arms of Hussey, becoming Gerald Strong-Hussey. From Gerald, Westown passed to his son Anthony, then his son Malachi, then his son Anthony Aloysius Strong-Hussey.

Vaulted basement

Anthony Aloysius Strong-Hussey, born on 21 June 1850, married Mary, daughter of Richard Henry Sheil of Liverpool and they had one daughter, Mary Mabel. Anthony and Mary Strong-Hussey became the best-known residents of Westown. In their time it was described as the finest mansion in Fingal. The house had thirty-two rooms, and in the basement three large kitchens produced enough food for the family and numerous guests. The servants' quarters consisted of a dining room and various sitting rooms and bedrooms. On the first floor, the front door led into a spacious hall with doors off to two large drawing rooms, a dining room and a parlour. The third floor held various bedchambers and the whole house was furnished in the finest possible manner.

View of house from northeast

The Westown estate, as was usual in its day, was mostly self-sufficient. Orchards and a walled garden provided fruit and vegetables. Hens, ducks, geese, turkeys, pheasants, rabbits, cattle, pigs and horses were kept in numerous farm buildings.

Mrs Hussey was an accomplished horse rider and a member of the Fingal Harriers, and she bred and trained horses for hunting. Part of the Westown estate was also given over for fox cover.

The 1911 census records the inhabitants of Westown House as: Anthony Hussey, aged 60; his wife, Mary Hussey, aged 53; their daughter, Mary Mabel Hussey, aged 24; and mother-in-law Teresa Sheil, aged 77. The Husseys had a staff of four: Ellen Jones, aged 20, maid; Susan Smyth, aged 22, parlour maid; Ann Doran, aged 59, cook; and Millicent Counell, aged 24, maid.

Mary Mabel married Colonel John Lockley Joseph Whitgreave in Naul Church on 5 August 1920. The reception was a truly lavish event, where hundreds of guests danced and celebrated through the night.

View from ground floor

The death of Anthony Hussey, buried in Naul Cemetery, brought about the final days of the Westown estate. His wife, Mary, retired from her job as a teacher in 1940 and went to live with her daughter in Liverpool. All but a few of the 435 acres of the Westown estate were sold to the Land Commission, which then divided up the land among local farmers.

Mary kept Westown House and a few acres until 1942, when Mr Cooney, a Drogheda coal merchant, became the new resident. Later residents were Mr P. J. Fogarty, TD from Swords, and then the Martin family. Mary Hussey died on 8 March 1948 at the age of 88 and is buried in Liverpool.

Eventually Westown House was abandoned and fell into total ruin. Local tradition tells of a guest who fell from a window. The following morning he was found lying dead in a pool of blood. His ghost is reputed to haunt the crumbling walls still.

Interior doorway with surviving plasterwork behind

View from basement looking upwards to chimney

County Galway

Bunowen Castle

In the sixteenth century Bunowen Castle, a smaller and more defensive structure than the current castle, was home to Donal O'Flaherty, chieftain of the O'Flaherty clan. He was a brutal man who was considered to be a good match for his wife, Gráinne Ní Mháille or Grace O'Malley, whom he had married when she was just 16 years old. Over the following years Grace took over the captaincy of the O'Flaherty fleet and took charge of most of the clan's political and business dealings.

When her husband was killed in an attack by the Joyce clan, her two sons denied Grace the O'Flaherty properties. As a consequence she made her new home on Clare Island in Clew Bay, where through protection and piracy she became supremely wealthy and famously known as the Pirate Queen.

View of castle from northeast

Bunowen Castle stayed in the hands of the O'Flahertys until it was taken by Cromwell in 1642. In County Westmeath, Arthur Geoghegan also had his family estates taken by Cromwell. During the war, however, Geoghegan's wife had provided protection for some of Cromwell's soldiers. For this unpatriotic act she received the grant of Bunowen Castle and thus the Geoghegans were transplanted from Westmeath into Galway.

The Geoghegans married into the Blake family of Galway. Charles Geoghegan of Bunowen married Mary, daughter of Valentine Blake of Drum, County Galway. Charles's son and heir, Edward Geoghegan, married Cecilia, daughter of Richard Blake of Ardfry, County Galway.

Internal view of castle tower

On 13 February 1808 John David Geoghegan of Bunowen petitioned King George III, and when His Majesty was satisfied that Geoghegan was paternally descended from Niall of the Nine Hostages, Geoghegan was granted royal licence and authority to take the name O'Neill, becoming John David O'Neill. His son and heir, Augustus John O'Neill, succeeded to the Bunowen estates on the death of his father in 1830.

Internal view showing arched top storey

101

From ground level looking up to chimney

View of side wing

Augustus, a magistrate for County Galway and also MP for the borough of Kingston-upon-Hull rebuilt Bunowen Castle into his mansion house; however, the construction became a considerable financial burden. In 1853 Augustus sold the Bunowen estate to Valentine O'Connor Blake of Towerhill, County Mayo (see p. 238) who used Bunowen as his summer residence. In 1909 much of the Blakes' Galway property was sold to the Congested Districts Board.

In the 1911 census the occupants of Bunowen Castle are recorded as: Thomas Joseph Blake, aged 61, Barrister of Law, not practicing; John Burke, aged 74, lodger and labourer; Anne Cooke, aged 27, general servant; and Norah Lanery, aged 15, kitchen girl.

Bunowen Castle is now long abandoned. All trace of the castle interior has disappeared with the ravages of Atlantic storms.

County Galway

Castle Daly

The Castle Daly estate was bought by Peter Daly in 1829; previously it had been called Corbally Castle, a residence of the Blakes since 1679. Peter Blake, third son of Sir Richard Blake of Ardfy, was granted the castle and lands of Corbally in the barony of Tiaquin, County Galway, on 20 December 1679. Peter Blake died in 1712 and was succeeded by his son, Patrick Blake. In 1757 Patrick Blake married Mary, daughter of John Morgan of Monksfield (see p. 124). Patrick Blake died in 1805 and was succeeded by his daughter, Charlotte, who married John Blake of Towerhill (see p. 238). Their son, Peter Blake, inherited the Corbally estate and subsequently sold it to Peter Daly in 1829.

View from garden entrance of house

Peter Daly had made his fortune in the West Indies and Daly's Grove in Jamaica is named after him. He rebuilt Corbally Castle as his Galway mansion house, planted the hill slopes with elegant trees and renamed the property Castle Daly. The house had fifty-two windows with the doorway lit from above by a large semicircular window. The wings of the house, one of which included the walls of the original Corbally Castle, were finished off with battlements to give the appearance of fortified towers.

Peter Daly's son, James Peter Daly, succeeded to the Castle Daly estate. He was born in March 1808, held the office of Justice of the Peace and Deputy Lieutenant for County Galway and became High Sheriff of County Galway in 1853. James Dermot Daly inherited Castle Daly when his father died in 1881.

The 1911 census shows the twenty-three rooms of Castle Daly occupied only by the caretaker John Forde and his wife, Bridget. The Daly family were in possession of Castle Daly until the 1940s.

Castle Daly was later demolished but, like some strange folly, the facade was left standing.

It is said that on a calm night, the ghostly sounds of the last ballroom dance can still be heard echoing across the Castle Daly demesne.

The Daly family motto, *Deo et regi fidelis*, translates as 'Loyal to God and King'.

Interior view of tower looking upwards

View through window to castle grounds

View of connecting passage which led to main house

View of tower dating to Corbally Castle, which was incorporated into Castle Daly

Castlegrove House

Castlegrove Castle, built by the De Burgos in the fifteenth century, fell to Cromwell in 1651. Cromwell's benefactors lived in the castle for a short while until the castle and lands came into the hands of the Blakes of Tuam, County Galway.

In the nineteenth century, Edward Blake, High Sheriff for County Galway, set about building himself a magnificent mansion house on the lands. Workers constructing the mansion house were paid 8d for unskilled labour and 1s 4d for skilled labour per working day of eleven hours.

When complete, the house of cut and carved stone was filled with the most splendid furniture of the time. The dining room measured 34 x 22 feet, the ballroom 36 x 22 feet, and there was also a drawing room, anteroom, study, a handsome hall with fireplace, an oak staircase and numerous bedrooms. The house was described as having every requisite and convenience usual in a modern first-rate residence.

360° view of remaining house interior

Edward Blake, by all accounts a gentleman except in the area of morality, was considered to be the finest driver of a carriage and horses in the whole province of Connacht. He once drove a carriage and pair at full speed from the Square in Tuam, down Shop Street, turning at the bridge and back again to the Square without slackening a rein. It was said he could whip a fly off his horse's nose at the full length of his whip without his horse being in the least disturbed.

Blake found that the main road from Tuam ran too close to his house and noise from passing traffic disturbed his privacy so he came up with a scheme. His men were sent to work constructing a new road further out from his house. When the new road was complete, early one morning, trees were felled at each end of the old road and his men sent out to direct passing traffic along the newly constructed road. Finding the new road an improvement the drivers soon ignored the old road, leaving Edward Blake free to gate off the old road and ensure his privacy.

Sketch from an early photograph

Edward Blake, however, overstretched himself and his grandiose schemes ended up bankrupting him. He turned to moneylenders and eventually in 1853 the house and lands were put up for sale by auction.

John Canon, a weaver's son from Eyrecourt, County Galway, paid £15,750 and became the new owner of the estate. Hence it was said that the great Edward Blake was driven from Castlegrove by one cannon without firing a shot. Blake moved to Dublin, where he died in 1873.

View to the rear of the house

The southwest corner of the house

Castlegrove Castle, also known as Feartagar Castle and as Jennings Castle, built some 400 years before Castlegrove House. It is in Irish State care.

Castlegrove brought John Canon no happiness: he suffered from various complaints, which led to him spending much time aboard his yacht and he rarely set foot on land. Finally Mr Canon ended his life by shooting himself. The Castlegrove estate was left to Mr Canon's agent, Mr Lewin, who lived at Castlegrove until July 1922, when, during the Irish Civil War, the house was attacked, set on fire and burnt to the ground. Local tradition is that Mr Lewin escaped through a secret passage, got on a train and was never seen again.

The Castlegrove estate was divided by the Land Commission in 1930. Over the years, much of the fine cut stone and anything useful was removed from the house. Today, trees and undergrowth have wrapped themselves around Edward Blake's magnificent mansion. All that remains are a few crumbling walls. The portico columns lie broken and collapsed. Fig trees, pear trees and raspberry bushes still give some indication of its glorious past.

◁ Corner of house with large bay window to side

▽ Garden lodge with Gothic windows

County Galway
Castlemoyle

Entrance hall looking towards front door

In 1677 Thomas Deane was granted more than 1,500 acres in County Galway, including the estates of Castlemoyle and Toghermore.

Castlemoyle House was built around 1770; however, by 1796 Ambrose Deane was bankrupt and the Browne family became the new occupiers. In 1820 Edward Browne of Castlemoyle was shot dead in his carriage while travelling in the area of Horseleap. It was said his murder had been the result of mistaken identity and that he had been confused for another man whose treatment of his tenants had made him a target.

View through basement window

In September 1849, John Browne of Castlemoyle, a sheriff of Galway, contracted cholera in Dublin. He continued his journey but died in Castlederry, County Cork, shortly after.

In 1809 John Browne's daughter, Mary, married John Nolan, and they had a son, also called John Nolan. John's fifth child, Sebastian Michael Nolan, a wealthy bachelor, bought Castlemoyle House and became the new resident until the late 1880s.

Interior view from basement

By 1911 Castlemoyle House was ruined and unoccupied. The Whelan family owned the estate and lived in a farmhouse adjoining the Castlemoyle stables. The census records the occupants as Patrick Whelan, aged 71, his two sons, two daughters and nephew.

Today the farmhouse is also in ruins; the only occupants of the once busy estate are the cattle, which quietly graze the old demesne.

◀ Partly bricked-up rear entrance to house

▼ Yard and farmhouse to rear of Castlemoyle

Monksfield House

The Morgan family, Cromwellian settlers originating from Wales, acquired the Monksfield estate in the seventeenth century. Morgan had also been granted other lands in County Galway including an old castle which was used as the Galway gaol. According to records the gaol consisted of a squalid two rooms with no fireplace. Its prisoners had few comforts.

On the Monksfield estate the Morgans set about building a home befitting their standing. Three storeys high over a large basement, their mansion house was soon complete.

In his *Topographical Dictionary* of 1837, Lewis records Captain Morgan as being resident at Monksfield.

360° view of front entrance, main staircase can
be seen to the right of photograph

The Monksfield estate passed from Charles Morgan to McNamara Morgan, then to Patrick Peter Morgan.
By the 1850s the Morgans had become so indebted that the estate was sold off to Thomas Shawe-Taylor.

By 1906 Monksfield had become the residence of Walter Shawe-Taylor but around 1908, after persistent
problems with his tenants, the estate was divided and sold off.

The house was inhabited well into the twentieth century but is now long abandoned; it stands on the
edge of a field, the plough passing a few feet from its door.

Front entrance with steps removed

View of house from southeast

Front room with recess in rear wall

Collapsed ceiling of drawing room

County Kerry

Ballycarbery Castle

Tradition relates that Ballycarbery Castle was the fortress of Carbery O'Shea, whose tomb can be found close by on the Atlantic shoreline. It is said bullock's blood was used to bind the lime and stone used in the castle's construction, a magic designed to make the castle impregnable.

From 1350 the castle become home to the O'Connells, who held it as wardens for their overlords, the MacCarthy clan.

Ballycarbery Castle stands close to Laght Point,
a few miles from Cahersiveen

It was said two O'Connell brothers occupied the castle, Seán in the higher levels, and Morgan in the lower. One day when the MacCarthy Mór and his lady came visiting, they were entertained in the higher levels of the castle by Seán. The next day, Morgan invited his lord to dine with him in the lower section of the castle. Seán thought his brother's gloomy lower area of the castle unfitting for the MacCarthy Mór

Partly damaged vaulted room on ground floor

The castle ruin contains many
narrow dark passageways

One of the mural stairways

View of castle from west

and an argument ensued; the MacCarthy Mór intervened, saying he would dine with whomever had the feast prepared first. Morgan quickly had all passages and doors to the higher section of the castle barred. No water or fuel could be brought to Seán's kitchens. Seán, however, had his meat boiled in Spanish wine, using the fierce-burning liquorice root for fuel. His feast was therefore prepared first and the honour of entertaining the MacCarthy Mór was his. Morgan O'Connell of Ballycarbery was later noted as a High Sheriff of County Kerry.

In 1596, when Donal MacCarthy, MacCarthy Mór and Earl of Clancar, died without an heir, Ballycarbery Castle passed into the hands of Sir Valentine Browne.

In the eighteenth century the castle was extended by the addition of a manor house built on to the west wall of the castle bawn. It is depicted as such in two nineteenth-century watercolours by artist Daniel Grose. This house was inhabited by the Lauder Family until it was demolished in the early twentieth century.

Around 1908 Mr Lynch wrote in the local press about an act of vandalism occurring at the fine old ruin of Ballycarbery Castle. The tenant occupying the adjoining farm had dismantled 25 feet of the castle's outer wall and removed a large quantity of loose stone. The tenant was cautioned against any further interference with the castle and the landowner Sir Morgan O'Connell agreed that the castle should be placed in State care. It is today overseen by the Office of Public Works.

According to local lore the castle was the site of many executions. It is said one of the victims, Morgan Dubh, can still be heard screaming on the darkest of winter nights.

County Kerry
Carhen House

Carhen House is close to the main road, a mile or two out of Cahersiveen

The tumbledown ruin of Carhen House, found on the outskirts of Cahersiveen, was once the family home of the O'Connells and on 6 August 1775 became the birthplace of Daniel O'Connell.

Daniel O'Connell was the eldest son of Morgan O'Connell, gentleman farmer of Carhen House. Daniel spent his youth in the Carhersiveen area until 1790 when his uncle, Maurice 'Hunting Cap' O'Connell of Derrynane, paid for Daniel to be schooled in France. From France, Daniel went on to study in London and then Dublin. By the time he qualified as a barrister in 1798 O'Connell was a campaigner for religious tolerance, freedom of conscience, democracy and the separation of Church and State. O'Connell spent the next ten years residing at Derrynane.

By 1815 O'Connell had become heavily involved in politics and was acknowledged as leader of the Catholic Emancipation movement. In 1823 he formed the Catholic Association. O'Connell stood for election to parliament for County Clare in 1828 and secured a massive victory. O'Connell, however, refused to take the Oath of Allegiance to the British Crown and since he had 6 million supporters, the British government became fearful of a nationwide uprising and eventually granted Catholic Emancipation in 1829. O'Connell became an Irish hero and earned the name 'The Liberator'. Later that year, he became the first Catholic in modern history to take a seat in the London parliament.

Remains of front entrance

O'Connell gave up his position as a barrister and focused full time on politics. His Repeal Association, campaigning for the repeal of the Act of Union and the establishment of an Irish parliament, drew a crowd of 750,000 people to the Hill of Tara.

By 1845 the Great Famine had struck. O'Connell devoted all his efforts to appealing for aid from the London parliament but little help was forthcoming, and the Famine devastated the Irish countryside. Before the potato crops returned, 1 million people had starved to death, and 1 million had emigrated. As a result all momentum for political reform was lost.

O'Connell, then elderly, suffering from exhaustion and in poor health, decided to make a pilgrimage to Rome. On his journey, arriving in Paris, he was cheered by vast crowds and described as the most successful champion of liberty and democracy in Europe. He never completed his journey and died in Genoa on 15 May 1847. At the request of O'Connell his heart was buried in Rome and his body in Dublin. His tomb in Glasnevin cemetery is surmounted by the tallest round tower in Ireland and it was restored and opened to the public in 2009.

The old O'Connell home slowly crumbles and cows wander freely around the ivy-covered walls. Daniel O'Connell's latter-day home, Derrynane House, however, fares a lot better than his birthplace. It is an Irish National Monument.

County Kerry
Castlequin

Castlequin was home to the Mahony family until early in the twentieth century. The Castlequin Mahonys are believed to be descended from Kean O'Mahony, of Kinalmeaky, chief of Carbery. Kean O'Mahony had forfeited his estates when he was implicated in the Tyrone Rebellion. Kean O'Mahony and his seven sons found themselves then removed to County Kerry.

By 1812 Myles Mahony was resident at Castlequin House, which at that time was quite a simple structure. Myles married Alice, daughter of John O'Connell of Derrynane, and around 1839 the house was

Interior of entrance porch with curious onlooker

rebuilt and enlarged by Myles' son, Kean Mahony, who became High Sheriff for County Kerry in 1840.

The new Castlequin House was a large two-storey, neo-Gothic house, built with a chapel in the west wing and a wine store in the opposite wing. The Gothic-style chapel was presided over by the Mahonys' own private family chaplain, Rev. Edward Flaherty. The Gothic features were carried through to the extensive outbuildings behind the house.

The remains of the private chapel

Kean Mahony had a large family. His first son, Myles, inherited the Castlequin estate; three other sons chose a military career: Lieutenant Colonel Daniel who served in the 58th Foot Regiment, Captain Denis who served in the French Irish Brigade and Darby, an officer, who died in Jamaica. Three of Kean's other children – John, Florence and Maurice – were drowned in a boating accident. His three daughters, Mary, Elizabeth and Gobinet, all married cousins. Castlequin was passed down the Mahony family until the early twentieth century.

View to front entrance

View of front room

Connecting corridor to private chapel
(there were several stages of building
modification in this area of the house)

Outbuildings to rear of house with
Gothic windows

In February 1918 Castlequin received some rare visitors: a pair of Great Spotted Cuckoos *(Clamator glandarius)* were seen by John Mahony on his farm. The species was verified by Mr O'Driscoll and recorded in the *Irish Naturalist Journal*, according to whose records there had only ever been one previous recorded sighting in Ireland. Unfortunately, a few days later, Mr O'Driscoll visited Mahony's farm and found the birds dead, apparently having suffered from exposure and starvation.

The Rosney family became residents until the house was sold in 1934, after which it fell into ruin.

Today the Castlequin demesne is silent, the house an empty shell, with cattle grazing over the old lawns and passing through the remains of the house and chapel as they please. The orange glow across the failing stonework is the result of yellow scales lichen *(xanthoria parietina)*, the propagation of which is encouraged by the warm Kerry climate.

The Mahony family motto *'Laisair romhuin a buadh'* translates as 'The torch that leads on to victory'.

County Kildare

Carbury Castle

The plaque shows the Colley coat of arms, with the text underneath: 'This Monument was Erected by Henry Colley Esq. in Memory of his Fathr Dudley Colley (alias) Cowley Esq. Son of Sr Henry, great Grand son of Sr Henry Cowley of Carbery Kt., who built this chappel & Burial Place for his Family and are Interred therein with their Wives Ann Warren daughter of Henry Warren of Grangebeg, Esq, & Katherine Cusach dauter of Sr Thomas Cusach Kt., then Ld Deputy of Ireland. Sr Henry Cowley was knighted by Queen Elizth in ye 2nd Year of her Reign, & made one of her Mai most Noble privy Council. Henry Colley (now living) son of Dudley married Mary Usher & had issue by her 6 sons & 6 Daughters, whereof 2 sons Henry & Richard & 6 daughters are now living; she was ye only Daughter of Sr William Usher of Bridg foot, Kt., by his lady Ursula ft Barb & lieth here interred for whose memory this Monument was made ye 10th of July Anoque Dom. 1705'.

Cairbre, son of Niall of the Nine Hostages, fifth-century King of Ireland, settled around the present-day hill of Carbury, giving his Anglicised name to the locality: the barony of Carbury.

Carbury Castle, shouldering the crest of the ancient hill, was originally built by the Bermingham family, descendants of Pierce de Bermingham, one of the early Anglo-Norman settlers of Ireland. Over the following centuries the castle was constantly a scene of strife, with the English barons within the Pale continually at war with the western Irish clans. It is recorded that, in 1475, Red Hugh O'Donnell demolished and burned Carbury Castle. It was plundered again in 1546 by Irish insurgents: the O'Kellys, the Maddens and the O'Connors.

In 1541 William de Bermingham was created Baron of Carbury but his son, Sir Edward de Bermingham, died without an heir and the title became extinct.

Carbury Castle was granted to the Colley family in 1562 since Captain Henry Colley had served in Queen Elizabeth's Irish army. The castle was modernised and extended by the Colleys with the addition of wings to the original rectangular structure. The eastern wing, added in the seventeenth century, included four remarkable chimney stacks and large mullioned windows.

When Captain Henry Colley's descendant, also Henry Colley, died in 1723 he left one son, another Henry Colley, and two daughters. The son died as a small child, leaving his sister Mary to inherit the Carbury estate. When Mary married Arthur Pomeroy in 1747 the castle thus passed to the Pomeroy family.

In the late 1700s Arthur Pomeroy abandoned Carbury Castle and built a modern mansion house, Newberry Hall, on the edge of the Carbury estate. This house still stands today. Arthur went on to become

Internal view of castle showing the remarkable chimney stacks

Carbury Castle looks out over an eight-eenth-century graveyard

Lord Harberton in 1787 and Viscount Harberton in 1791. Carbury Castle was left to crumble, leaving the remarkable chimney-stacked ruin which stands on the site today. The Colley family mausoleum is located in a graveyard a short distance from the castle ruin.

Trinity Well, found at the foot of Carbury Hill, is the source of the River Boyne. According to legend the well once had remarkable powers: any person other than the King who approached the well was instantly deprived of sight, with their eyes bursting horrendously. Boan, the queen, was determined to test the mystical powers of the water and one day she not only approached the well, but circled it three times, upon which the ancient charm was broken. The spring burst open and an enormous wave crashed down upon Queen Boan. The rushing water drowned her and carried her body along the course of what is now the River Boyne and swept her out to sea. Queen Boan thus gave her name to the River Boyne. Each year on Trinity Sunday a pattern day is celebrated at Trinity Well. Mass is offered and a parade and festival occur in the adjoining field.

Donore House

When Thomas Wentworth, Earl of Stafford, became Lord Deputy of Ireland in 1633, he set about buying up the lands of County Kildare and acquired more than 5,000 acres. Wentworth had to pay heavily: the price for the Donore estate was reputed to be £4 per acre, while the equivalent in County Wicklow was only 16 shillings. His mission in Ireland was to increase royal revenue, but he did not neglect his own personal fortunes and went on to create many enemies. In 1641 he was summoned to London

Internal view of back door from basement level

to face the charge of treason. He defended himself successfully but his enemies in the London parliament sought a Bill of Attainder, whereby with the signature of Charles I, Wentworth was declared guilty without trial and then executed on 12 May 1641 in front of a crowd of 200,000 on Tower Hill.

The Crown regranted Thomas Wentworth's estates to his eldest son, William, and the Donore estate was leased to Walter Hussey. These lands were described as 'one castle with a demolished hall thereto adjoining'

In 1750 Walter Hussey's descendant, Edward Hussey, mortgaged the Donore Estate. He obtained £6,000 and began building the Donore mansion house. In 1753 the mortgage was repaid; however, in 1757 the estate was mortgaged by Elizabeth Hussey for £4,500 to Doctor Barnard, Lord Bishop of Derry. Elizabeth Hussey died in the same year, leaving her son Walter to inherit the mortgaged Donore estate. Walter Hussey went on to take the name Burgh from his cousin Richard Burgh, as a condition to inherit half of his cousin's Limerick estate, becoming Walter Hussey-Burgh.

The completed Donore mansion was a magnificent 'U' plan house, two storeys over basement, and entered through a pedimented Ionic doorcase in a central three-sided bow. Several rooms led off from a central hallway: a dining room, study, drawing room, library, kitchen, cellar, wine cellar and four other large reception rooms. A grand staircase led up to the first floor, which contained at least nine bedchambers. The whole house was furnished in the finest possible fashion.

Tree growing through the back door

The few remaining traces of the interior are being slowly
dislodged by invading roots and vines

157

Remains of cantilevered stone staircase

Close-up of stair remains

View from front entrance hall with overgrown door at centre leading to main staircase

Walter Hussey-Burgh was called to the Irish Bar in 1769 and went on to become one of the most eloquent and charismatic lawyers in Ireland. In 1777 he was appointed Prime Sergeant and in 1782 Chief Baron of the Exchequer. He died in 1783, aged 41, leaving four daughters and one son. It was said that, although very successful, Walter Hussey-Burgh had an expensive lifestyle. The family's finances were left in a difficult position. In 1796, the executors of Dr Barnard sued Walter's son, Rev. John Hussey-Burgh, for the money due to them from the 1757 mortgage. A court subsequently ordered that the Donore estate be offered for public sale. On 22 January 1800 the house was sold for £14,150. However, it was the Hussey-Burgh family who bought their own house. Dr Barnard's executors received £5,762 and the mortgage on the house was repaid.

In 1810 Rev. John Hussey-Burgh let the house and estate to Philip Roche; the Roche family was to hold the estate for three lives at the yearly rent of £500. Rev. John Hussey-Burgh took up residence at the humbler Dromkeen House, County Limerick, which his father had inherited from a cousin.

When Philip Roche died, his son John took up residence at Donore. When John Roche died in 1830 the Donore lease was surrendered and the house again occupied by the Hussey-Burghs. However, the house was hugely expensive to run, and in 1850 it was vacant and then let to a series of tenants: firstly Rev. Elis Archer and Rev. Mr. Gilmore, then Mr Edward Morrin. In 1874 all the Hussey-Burghs' Kildare property passed to Mr James Kelly. In 1911 the estate was divided and sold to its tenants under the Land Purchase Act and Mrs Maria Morrin acquired some 434 acres.

By 1956 the Donore mansion house was no longer habitable; the house was too large and uncongenial for a farming family. The Morrin family built a modern comfortable residence and abandoned the old mansion house. They still farm the Donore estate today.

View of aligning doorways

Water pump at rear of house

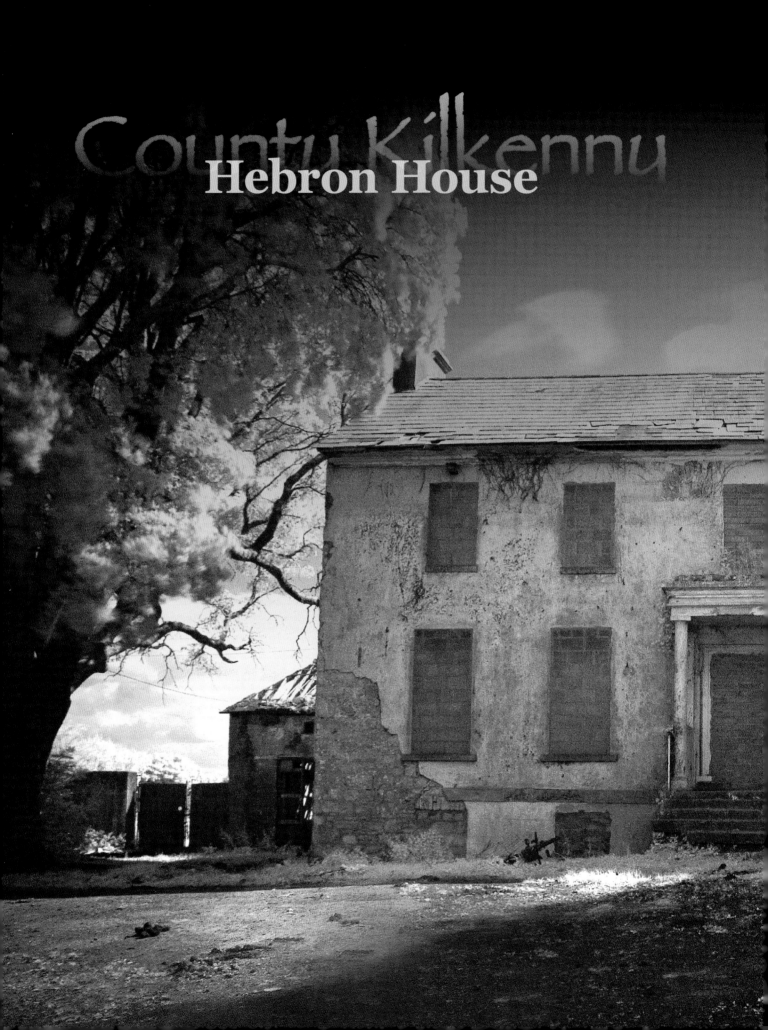

County Kilkenny

Hebron House

The Helsham family, originally of Sussex, England, came to Ireland in the seventeenth century and settled in the Kilkenny area. Joshua Helsham was Mayor of Kilkenny in 1692 and 1693. Joshua's descendant Richard Helsham, at the age of 15, had gone from Kilkenny College to study as a physician at Trinity College, Dublin. Richard Helsham went on to become a medical doctor, Senior Fellow and Professor of Physic at Trinity College. When Richard Helsham retired, he returned to Kilkenny and bought a country residence. In 1737 he paid £800 for the purchase of 'House, Buildings, Watercourse, Common Woods,

View of house from the northeast

Underwoods etc' to Constance Deane, spinster, and became the owner of the Hebron estate.

Richard, however, did not have long to enjoy his new mansion. He died just one year later in 1738. His will stipulated that 'his body be carried to the place of burial by the light of one taper only at the dead of night without Herse or Pomp, attended by my domestics only'. *The Gentlemen's Magazine* noted that 'he desired his body might be opened for the benefit of mankind'. He was interred at St Mary's Churchyard, Dublin.

Hebron was inherited by Richard Helsham's nephew, also named Richard Helsham, who served as

Wallpapered front rooms filled with debris

164

Collapsed stairway

a city Sheriff in 1740 and 1741. In the early 1800s Hebron House was let to George Cronyn. In 1833 following the death of Cronyn, a public auction was held at the house, and then it was advertised to let, after which the house was occupied by Lieutenant Colonel Jones.

In 1854 the house was sold to Michael Murphy, who had returned to Ireland from Australia.

The 1911 census records Michael Murphy's son and two daughters occupying the seventeen rooms of Hebron House: Thomas E. Murphy, aged 45, farmer and single; Mary Murphy, aged 42; and Gertrude Murphy, aged 38. The Murphys occupied Hebron until 1953, when they retired to St Michaels, adjoining High Park Convent, Dublin. Hebron House was then sold to John Mansfield.

In 1998 Hebron House and lands were sold for £1.74 million. In 2005 it was subject to a planning application to be restored and refurbished for use as a hotel, with further expansion of 208 bedrooms.

Today the house stands quiet, windows and doors are bricked up, and horses are left to graze peacefully over the formerly magnificent lawns.

Front drawing room with discarded modern furniture

County Kilkenny
Newtown Castle

Newtown was given its name by its first Anglo-Norman occupier, Baldwin de Hamptonsford. He was granted the lands in the early thirteenth century and called it *Nova Villa* or Newtown. Later the lands would pass to the D'Erleys and the parish became known as Earlstown.

The D'Erleys of Earlstown prospered and grew in importance. However, by the close of the fourteenth century the property of Earlstown and the title of Baron of Erley had passed to the Sweetman family. In 1360 Milo Sweetman was treasurer of Ossory and also elected Bishop of the diocese. His election, however, was cancelled by the Pope who instead appointed him Archbishop of Armagh.

In 1478, John Sweetman was chief lord of all the barony of Erley and by 1560 William Sweetman had become the largest freeholder in the barony of Kells, his estate then being valued at £74.

Newtown Castle was built by the Sweetmans around the year 1500. The castle was designed to impress rather than serve a purely military purpose; other than the murder hole above the entrance doorway, the castle had few defensive features. It was of four storeys. The upper floors were lit by both ogee-headed windows and rectangular single lights. The ground floor ceiling was vaulted, with the main living area of the castle above it. The top floor contained a secret chamber.

The Sweetmans held the manor of Earlstown until 1653 when William Sweetman took the side of the Confederate Catholics. He forfeited his estate under Cromwell and found himself transplanted to Connacht in 1654.

360° view of castle interior

The ruined Newtown Castle went on to serve as the Newtown district chapel until 1808. With no bell to give notice when Mass was due to commence, a local man – Bill Delany – was employed to call to the congregation. It was said he was blessed with a voice with no rival in Ireland. He would ascend to the top of the castle and give full vent to his vocal powers. His call echoed near and far through the neighbourhood so well that the makeshift chapel never failed to be filled to capacity. In 1809 Newtown chapel was built by Fr Forrestall and Delany's service was no longer needed.

Though ruined, Newtown Castle still stands as a fine example of the Irish tower house.

Castle top floor interior

Castle interior passageway

County Kilkenny
Newtown House

The Sweetmans had held the manor of Earlstown until 1653 when William Sweetman took the side of the Confederate Catholics. Sweetman forfeited his estate under Cromwell and found himself transplanted to Connacht in 1654. The Newtown estate eventually came into the hands of the Earl of Carrick.

When Henry Thomas Butler, the second Earl of Carrick, died in 1813 his estates of Mount Juliet and Newtown were passed to his daughter's husband, the Honourable Charles Harward Butler-Clarke-Southwell-Wandesforde. When Charles married Lady Sarah Butler, he took her name as a condition of his inheritance. His other surnames had also been taken with various other inheritances. He resided at Mount Juliet, while the Newtown estate was let to several tenants.

360° view of corridor and back rooms

In 1834 the Rev. Benjamin Morris, rector of Rincurran, was occupying Newtown House. He died in 1846. In the 1911 census, the occupants are recorded as: the widow Louisa Smithwick, aged 61; her son George Smithwick, aged 36, retired brewer; and daughter Louisa Smithwick, aged 38. The Smithwicks had a staff of four: Statia Byrne, aged 18, domestic servant; Ada Roche, aged 19, domestic servant; Nicholas Bolger, aged 18, stable boy; and Edward Daly, aged 18, stable boy. There were also two visitors in the house at the time: Helen Fleming, aged 31 and Arthur Caren, aged 3.

Front entrance with pediment and doorcase missing

Front hall with recess in rear wall

View to outbuildings at rear of house

Louisa Smithwick had been married to Daniel O'Connell Smithwick who died on 19 October 1883. The Smithwick brewery is the oldest operating brewery in Ireland. It was founded by John Smithwick in 1710, and was expanded by Daniel O'Connell Smithwick's father, Edmund Smithwick. By 1920 Smithwick's beer was the largest selling ale brand in Ireland, a position it still holds to this day. No wonder George Smithwick could afford to retire from the brewing business at the age of 36. In 1965, Smithwick's became a public company as part of Irish Ale Breweries and in the same year, Arthur Guinness Son and Company (Dublin) Ltd took financial control of the operation. Today both Guinness and Smithwick's are under the control of Diageo.

By 1969 the roof of Newtown House had been removed to avoid various property taxes. The house then fell into total ruin.

Front rooms

Bellegrove House was built around the year 1835 by Mr George Adair. The Adair family is descended from Thomas, sixth Earl of Desmond. On one occasion the Earl was away in the country, undertaking a hunting expedition. At the end of the day he found himself quite lost and with the cold night drawing in on him he sought shelter and a bed for the night. He found comfortable accommodation at the residence of Mr William McCormic. A night of entertainment ensued, resulting in the subsequent marriage of the Earl to McCormic's daughter. The Earl's family was disgusted with his unsuitable choice for a wife, and he was forced to resign his title and estates to his younger brother. Two years later, in 1420, it was said he died

The impressive remains of Bellegrove House stand on the edge of a cornfield

of grief. The King of England attended his funeral. The Earl left two young children, whose descendants started new branches of the Adair family, first in Scotland and then in Ireland.

By 1800 George Adair was managing property for various English absentee landlords and had acquired his own considerable landholdings. He had earned a reputation for evicting tenant farmers from property to promote his own economic fortunes, an act for which his son, John George Adair, born 3 March 1823, would become notorious. George Adair died in 1873, leaving his son, John George Adair, to inherit the family fortune.

View of front entrance

Bellegrove House was originally built around three sides of an open entrance courtyard. The courtyard was later filled in and turned into a winter garden by Adair's wife, Cornelia. She was a wealthy widowed daughter of a family from upstate New York, whom Adair had met at a society ball. Cornelia's wealth helped create Glenveagh Castle, the Adairs' property in County Donegal. With money no object in her quest to improve Bellegrove House, Mrs Adair went on to add a huge conservatory made to the design of Sir Thomas Newenham Deane. The conservatory featured ornate terracotta columns which had been modelled on the columns of the Basilica of St John Lateran in Rome.

John George Adair rose to infamy when he evicted all the tenants from his Donegal estate at Glenveagh Castle, Derryveagh. On St Patrick's Day 1861, Adair arranged for 203 constables to forcibly remove all

Internal view of front bow

An underground corridor extends out from the basement, leading to storage rooms and on to the stable yard at the rear of the house

The basement rooms are connected by a rectangular corridor

of the forty-seven families who were tenants on his land. Two hundred and forty-four people ended up homeless and destined for the poorhouse or emigration. The Derryveagh Evictions became one of the most notorious stories of oppression by wealthy landlords in the history of Ireland.

John George Adair died in 1885 and was interred in Glenveagh. His wife had the face of a rock inscribed with his name and the words 'Brave, Just and Generous'. Shortly after, the rock was struck by lightning and broke into many pieces, which fell into the nearby lake.

Remains of basement kitchen fireplaces at bottom right

Bellegrove House was destroyed by accidental fire in 1887. Today only its walls remain. The magnificent Italianate facade gives some indication of the immense wealth of its nineteenth-century residents.

Bellegrove gate lodge fares little better than the main house

County Laois
Lea Castle

Charles of the Horses jumped his horse from this point:
he survived the fall, the horse did not

Lea Castle was built by the Anglo-Normans at the end of the twelfth century. The castle became a scene of constant warfare for the next four and a half centuries. O'More burned the castle in 1346 and in 1422 O'Dempsey captured it from the Earl of Kildare. The Earl of Ormond took it from the Earl of Kildare in 1452. The Earl of Kildare regained the castle in 1535. In 1556 it was mortgaged for £500 and 600 ounces of silver by the Earl to Sir Maurice Fitzgerald of Lackagh. In 1641 the castle was taken by the Irish under Henry O'Dempsey and then retaken by the Parliamentarians under Lord Lisle, and then

The remaining corner tower of Lea Castle rises above the undergrowth

again taken by the Confederates under Lord Castlehaven. The Confederates operated a mint in the castle, producing copper coins known as St Patrick's pence.

In 1650 the castle was again retaken by the Parliamentarians under Colonels Hewson and Reynolds. To prevent it being reoccupied the castle was first dismantled and then sections of the walls blown up with gunpowder. The castle had consisted of a quadrangle building of three storeys flanked by round bastions. At the rear of the castle was an inner court. The outer entrance to the castle consisted of a gate and barbican defended by a portcullis, also flanked by round bastions. In 1712 this outer entrance became home to Hector Graham. Graham had a large house and estate in County Monaghan but instead he chose a solitary, comfortless existence. He repaired a small portion of the castle, forming it into his home.

Graham was reputed to be a fine horseman. On one occasion just as he reached the castle gate he heard a shriek echoing faintly in the distance. He put his spurs to his mare and set off at full gallop, leaping every fence, hedge and ditch that he met. He soon came across a local girl who was being set about by a bunch of ruffians. Graham leapt from his horse and using his heavy hunting whip, scattered the villains within minutes. Graham returned the poor girl unharmed to her father.

Cahir na gCapall or Charles of the Horses, a horse thief famous across seven counties and the scourge of every sheriff in Ireland, had been known to keep his stolen herd in the overgrown vaults of the Lea Castle ruin. On one occasion, he was cornered at the entrance to his secret stable. A sheriff and his party of men held a warrant for his immediate arrest. Charles boldly rode up the steep, narrow staircase built into the Lea Castle wall. The sheriff and his men dismounted and followed up on foot. Charles, seeing no other means for escape, forced his horse to leap from the platform at the top of the stairs. The fall of more than 100 feet killed the animal instantly; Charles, however, forced himself to his feet and staggered to the edge of the River Barrow. As the sheriff's men came running he made his escape by diving into the water.

Hector Graham of Lea Castle also joined the sheriff's party of men and Charles of the Horses was soon captured. A few days later the desperado horse thief was tried and found guilty. He felt the hangman's noose tighten around his neck.

Today Lea Castle is silent. Grass, weeds and undergrowth slowly cover its fallen walls.

The castle walls have been battered by centuries of warfare

The staircase up which Charles of the Horses made his escape

Interior of corner tower, looking up

County Leitrim

Drumhierny Lodge

The Drumhierny estate was established by the La Touche family around the year 1800. David Digues La Touche des Rompieres, born in 1671 in the Loire Valley, France, had fled to Holland in search of religious freedom. He obtained a commission in General Caillemotte's Regiment, in the army of William of Orange. In 1690 David came to Ireland and fought in the Battle of the Boyne, where General Caillemotte was killed, and the Regiment disbanded. David went to Dublin where he set up a silk and cotton weaving business with another Huguenot. His business became a gathering place and as his business prospered, David went on to form a bank where he could advance loans to other Huguenot businessmen. In 1716

Front room showing collapsed floor joists from upper storey

he became a partner with Nathaniel Kane and the Kane–La Touche bank was formed. As the bank flourished, David bought plots of land around the St Stephen's Green/Aungier St area of Dublin. David died, leaving two sons, James and David. James took on the fabric side of the business, and David took on the bank. The La Touche Bank would later become the Bank of Ireland.

The younger David La Touche, like his father, also speculated in land purchase and bought large estates in counties Dublin, Carlow, Kildare, Leitrim, Tipperary and Wicklow. David's son, Peter, laid out extensive plantations on the Drumhierny estate and built Drumhierny Lodge.

View from porch into entrance hall

Drumhierny Lodge, a six-bay house, consisted of a porch, which led into a hallway; to the right of the hallway was a fine drawing room and to the left a dining room. The rear hall led to a kitchen, pantry and wine cellar. There were three other reception rooms used for various functions. On the first floor a master bedroom and seven other bedrooms all shared only one toilet. At one end of the house there was once a magnificent conservatory, of which no evidence remains. To the rear of the house were extensive stables and outbuildings.

Peter La Touche married the Honourable Charlotte Maude, and they had twelve children: nine boys and three girls. Drumhierny was occupied by a number of their sons. In 1856 the lodge was occupied by Francis La Touche, and on his death the property passed to his brother Major Octavius La Touche. Octavius derived his name from being Peter La Touche's eighth son. He died in 1897 leaving his estates to his wife, son and three daughters. In the 1911 census, Drumhierny is recorded as being owned by Octavius' daughter, Charlotte; however, the house was unoccupied.

On 2 April 1912 Drumhierny Lodge was sold by public auction to Mr Michael J. O'Connor, a Leitrim man who had made his fortune in America. O'Connor paid £3,000 for the house and 300 acres. When Michael died, Drumhierny was inherited by his daughter Marion, who married into the O'Rahily family. By the 1980s Drumhierny was abandoned.

Today, the forest slowly invades, the roof has long since collapsed and there is little evidence of the grandeur of this once fine residence.

View of front room interior

Chimney surround hanging from wall

County Leitrim
Lakefield House

Overgrown steps lead up to the front door

The Lakefield estate was established when Ann Crofton, daughter of Duke Crofton, married Randal Slack on 20 October 1754. Randal bought 57 acres from Edmund Armstrong in 1755 and took up residence at Lakefield with his wife. In those days Lakefield House was a simple structure; however, in 1771 the foundations for a new house were laid. It took forty-four years to complete the house, when the third Duke Crofton was in residence. This Duke Crofton was reputedly a small, stout man of immoral character. He was a captain in the Mohill Yeomanry and personally supervised the hanging of General

Blake, commander of the United Irishmen forces after the Battle of Ballinamuck, where the French and Irish forces fell to the British after the 1798 Rebellion.

Many years later a chest, full of beautifully crafted French pistols and rifles, was found in the cellar at Lakefield, which had been apparently taken from the French forces at Ballinamuck.

The Lakefield estate was extensively landscaped by the third Duke Crofton. It was said the demesne had many fine monkey puzzle trees and was amongst the finest in Ireland. Lakefield was inherited by the fourth Duke Crofton, then by Richard Henry Crofton, and then by Captain Duke Arthur Crofton.

Captain Duke Arthur Crofton served in the Royal Navy. He retired from service in 1887 and concentrated on farming at Lakefield where he had a special interest in fruit growing. During his time at Lakefield, the estate prospered. The Captain and his wife were very popular both with their tenants and the local gentry. Lakefield House was the setting for many parties and hosted game shoots in the shooting season. It was during one such shoot that Mrs Crofton's favourite dog was accidentally shot dead by her son. Mrs Crofton was so devastated that she had a plaque erected in its memory. The plaque can still be seen today 'A much loved dog, born 1893, died from an accident 4th June 1901'.

The 1911 census records the occupants of Lakefield House as: Duke Crofton, aged 60; his wife Maude Crofton, aged 56; their daughter Hilda Crofton, aged 16; and son Patrick Crofton, aged 11. The Croftons had a staff of six: Martie Parker, aged 35, governess; David King, aged 45, coachman; Kate Parkes, aged 30, cook; Mary O'Rourke, aged 28, housemaid; Elisabeth May, aged 25, parlour maid; and Maggie Byrne, aged 19, kitchen maid.

Although in his mid-sixties, the Captain insisted on joining the Red Cross during the First World War. He went to the Western Front where he died from pneumonia on 25 December 1918.

Mrs Crofton continued to live at Lakefield House until 1926 when she moved to live with her daughter Amy in England. Thereafter the house began to deteriorate.

The Land Commission purchased the Lakefield estate in 1931 and it was divided amongst local farmers. William Alphonsius Quinn became the new owner of the house in 1942. The trees on the estate were felled and sold for firewood. By 1957, Mr Quinn had died and the house was in ruins with the Lakefield estate barely recognisable.

The front door is locked and chained

The central stairway is open from the basement to the gaping roof

Timber window frames are still in place

The stairs have entirely collapsed

The yard behind the house features fine cut-stone outbuildings

Dromore Castle

William Hale John Charles Perry inherited the title of the Earl of Limerick from his grandfather in 1866. The Earls of Limerick had previously occupied a residence in Henry Street; however, William Hale John Charles Perry had more fanciful plans and decided to expand his grandfather's idea for a hunting lodge into a permanent residence. Being a patron of architecture he employed the leading English architect of the day, Edward William Godwin.

360° view of castle interior from first floor landing

Godwin came to Ireland in 1867 in order to inspect possible sites for the proposed new residence. The Earl himself spent many weary days searching for a site. When he brought Godwin to the top of Dromore Hill, the beauty of the scene laid out before them led to a quick decision. Godwin was said to have described the location, on the edge of a wood overlooking Dromore Lough, as 'dreamlike'. Seeking inspiration and to perfect his design, Godwin travelled across Ireland inspecting numerous medieval

View of courtyard from entrance

View of castle from southwest tower

castles and drew elements from many. In 1868 the building contract was appointed to an Englishman, under the supervision of a resident Clerk of Works. Any local man with a horse and cart could be employed from 7 a.m. to 7 p.m., drawing stones from the quarries in Foynes for a salary of four shillings per day. Work progressed slowly and was still ongoing two years later. However, when the contractor was awarded a new contract for the building of a church in County Clare, the castle was promptly completed. The cost to the Earl was said to be £100,000, which in those days was an enormous sum.

Godwin is reputed to have said of Dromore Castle that he had seen it by moonlight, seen it from the road at a distance from every angle, and the silhouette was about as charming a thing as ever he saw in his life.

The finished castle was considered to relate to no other castle in Ireland, the number of turrets and chimneys giving it the appearance of a fairy-tale castle more suited to the banks of the Rhine.

Soon after the Earl moved into his new residence, patches of damp started to appear. Eventually the magnificently decorated interior walls started to disintegrate as damp spread through the entire structure. Godwin was criticised for not having taken the damp climate into consideration. The situation was rectified and Dromore Castle remained home to the third Earl until his death in 1896.

The fourth Earl, an army man who gained the rank of captain and honorary major in the service of the 5th Battalion, Royal Munster Fusiliers, spent little time at Dromore. The castle was completely abandoned during the First World War and eventually sold to the McMahon family by the fifth Earl, Edmund Colquhoun Perry, in 1939. The McMahon family occupied the castle until 1950. When an attempt to find a buyer proved unsuccessful the castle was dismantled to avoid various property taxes.

In 1988 Dromore Castle was used as the location for the film *High Spirits*, starring Peter O'Toole, Daryl Hannah and Liam Neeson. Peter O'Toole plays the part of a financially troubled Irish nobleman who lives with his mother in a castle that is about to be repossessed. Desperate to raise money, he turns his castle into a haunted castle theme park. Plastic fake windows and other props from the filming can still be found lying in corners of the crumbling castle interior.

The current owner of Dromore Castle estate has transformed the castle stables into his family home. The castle itself is one of the most dramatic and remarkable ruins in the whole of Ireland.

View from ground level showing at least four storeys

Plastic prop windows left from shoot the film *High Spirits*

View from chapel floor to turret

The Grange

In 1790 Standish O'Grady purchased 110 acres of land in the area of The Grange. Standish first lived in a small old farmhouse while his neighbour Hugh Ingoldsby Massy had a fine mansion house that Standish wanted to purchase. This old mansion was also called The Grange and Massy would sell him only a life use of it. When Standish died, his son Thomas O'Grady inherited his father's estate, but had to give up the mansion house, whereon it passed to Count de Salis.

360° view of house interior

Standish O'Grady's brother, Nicholas, had been called to the Irish Bar. However, he found this did not suit his aspirations. He moved to London where he became a successful gambler and amassed a considerable fortune. He ended up in Paris where he committed suicide, leaving his fortune to his nephew, Thomas.

Thomas O'Grady, on inheriting his uncle's wealth, decided to build himself a fine new mansion, which he named The Grange, after the house rented by his father. The new Grange estate faced sloping

Ground floor window

View of house interior from basement cellar

View of house from southwest

View from ground floor looking up

down to a river; it was superbly planted and included a deer park. The house was three storeys over basement, six bays at the front and three bays on the side. At the rear of the house there was an extensive and elaborate set of stables and farm buildings.

When Thomas O'Grady died unmarried, The Grange was inherited by his sister, Margaret, who had married the Rev. Robert Croker, and thus The Grange came to the Croker family. Caroline Croker inherited the Grange estates. She was unmarried and lived in the house with a staff of seven servants.

The 1911 census records the occupant of The Grange as: Caroline Croker, aged 72. The house was staffed by: Annie Duff, aged 58, domestic servant; Mary Kirby, aged 39, cook; Ellen Murphy, aged 40, housemaid; Margaret Feston, aged 68, laundress; Bridget Higgins, aged 32, kitchen maid; Thomas Gabin, aged 42, coachman; and Patrick Cronin, aged 19, domestic servant.

By 1928 Caroline Croker had died unmarried and the estate, acquired by the Land Commission, was divided among local farmers. Around 1940 the house was dismantled: fireplaces, doors and anything else of use was removed. The house was stripped of its roof and left to fall into ruin.

Wine cellar

Outbuildings to rear of house

County Louth

Kilsaran House

Kilsaran House was built in 1780 by the Bellingham family of Castle Bellingham. The house was originally five bays at the front and four bays at the side with extensive outbuildings to the rear.

At the time of the house's construction the town of Kilsaran was famous for Castle-Bellingham Ale, deemed to be the best malt liquor in Ireland. The brewery had been built around 1770 by O'Bryen Bellingham and was the cause of considerable prosperity in the area.

360° view of house interior with dance hall through breach in wall to the right

In 1815 Kilsaran House became the summer home of George Vesey, who was Rector of Manfieldstown and who had a pew in Castle Bellingham church.

In 1837, Lewis records Kilsaran House as the home of M. Chester Esquire. Later the house would become home to John Chester, a leading magistrate of County Louth. When John Chester died, he left his

Old photograph showing the house before the dance hall was built

The 1911 census records Kilsaran House as owned by a Mr Walsh who was letting the house to the Jameson family. The occupants are recorded as: James Jameson, aged 55, artist and painter; his wife, Edith Jameson, aged 56; and their daughter, Ursula Jameson, aged 20. The house had a staff of three: Mary Kelly, aged 28, cook; Rose Tormey, aged 26, maid; and Lizzie Garland, aged 19, housemaid. The house also had a visitor: George Benson, aged 22, soldier, Second Lieutenant RFA. The Jamesons identify their religion as 'Church of England' whilst the servants' religion is described as 'Church of Rome'.

After 1920 Kilsaran House was home to James Chester Walsh. James married Freda Clarke in 1935 and they ran a busy farm. James, though, was not content with just his farming business and added a large ballroom to the side of the house. In 1933 James applied for a dance licence, which was objected to by the local priest, Father Callan. According to Father Callan, 'at the previous dance motorcars had been parked all around the place and a lot of larcenies had taken place'. James, however, insisted that his committee of local ladies was quite capable of supervising the dance to prevent any mischievous behaviour. A temporary licence was granted with the provision that no alcohol was served and one-quarter of all dances were Irish. The venue continued on as the best ballroom in the area but received considerable attention from Sergeant O'Connor and the High Court.

Ivy-covered house remains with concrete dance hall to right

When James died around 1967, Freda continued running the farm, and the ballroom was used by a local factory as a storage facility. The house gradually began to fall into disrepair and by the time Freda retired and moved to England in the 1990s it was almost uninhabitable.

During the late 1990s Kilsaran House once again became a venue for dances, in the form of rave parties. According to local sources the ballroom made a fantastic dance floor and the warren of derelict rooms in the house made for some great 'chill-out rooms'. The house was eventually destroyed by vandals and set on fire.

The remains of Kilsaran House and thirty-two acres were sold by auction on 12 May 1998 for £245,000. Today the ballroom still stands, although Kilsaran House is little more than a tumbledown ruin.

Dance hall with huge circular window to the rear

Collapsed interior structure

Old photograph of dance party in front of circular window

County Louth
Louth Hall

Oliver Plunkett (no connection to the Catholic Archbishop of Armagh of the same name, who was canonised in 1975) was created Baron of Louth by Henry VIII on 15 June 1541. At this time the Plunketts resided in a tower house at Tallanstown. The first Baron's son, Thomas, enlarged the tower house and planted woodland, in which it was said one could walk around for the whole day without walking over the same patch twice, or being exposed to sun or rain. The tower house became known as Louth Hall.

The Plunketts remained loyal to the English Crown until the rebellion of 1641 when the sixth Baron Louth, also Oliver Plunkett, formed an alliance with Irish rebel leaders from Ulster. In 1642 Plunkett

360° view: sections of the interior floor and walls still survive

was taken prisoner and outlawed for high treason. His lands were forfeited under the Cromwellian land settlement until 1660 when Charles II came to the throne, and the majority of his lands were restored.

In 1760 Thomas Oliver Plunkett, the eleventh Baron Louth, added a three-storey wing to Louth Hall. He also had the outlawry of his descendants overturned and in 1798, took his seat in the House of Lords.

In 1805 Richard Johnston, elder brother of the architect Francis Johnston, was employed to extensively remodel Louth Hall. The wing, added in 1760, was further extended to the rear and the height increased with the addition of battlements. The tower house was given pointed windows and other Gothic features

The small front door appears drastically out of proportion with the rest of the house

The entrance to the house was a small doorway with a fanlight, quite out of proportion with the rest of the house. Louth Hall, by all accounts, gave the effect of vastness and grimness.

In Lewis' *Topographical Dictionary* of 1837, it is noted that the Louth Hall demesne amounted to 250 acres and was well planted with trees, and that 'the estate included 700 acres of the best land in Ireland under tillage'. Lewis also wrote that 'the soil is generally good, and agriculture has greatly advanced, the resident gentry and farmers having exerted themselves to introduce the improved system both in the cultivation of land and in the rearing of cattle'. The whole estate at this time amounted to 3,068 acres.

In 1716 the estate had brought in a yearly rental of £1,700 from its various tenants and by 1830 this had increased to £4,499.

When the Land Purchase Act was introduced in 1903, negotiations immediately started between Lord Louth and his tenants. By 1909 most of the estate had been sold off. The Plunketts continued to hold the house and demesne but increasingly spent their time in England. The 1911 census records the house as being occupied by just two servants. When the fourteenth Baron Louth died in 1941 the house and all remaining lands were sold.

An upturned bath tub has found its way on to the rooftop

Another lost bath

In 1953 Louth Hall was considered for conversion into a Central Maternity Home; it was surveyed by the county engineer and reported as being generally sound, with the internal plastering fairly good, the stairs slightly out of level, the windows in need of overhauling, and the rooms generally damp because of condensation. The engineer considered that the aspect of the house was wrong – sixteen out of the twenty-two rooms were facing north – and that the cost of putting the building into good repair was prohibitive.

Louth Hall did not become a maternity home and instead was used by local farmers as a potato loft and grain store, eventually falling into total dereliction.

According to tradition, one Lord Louth was once summoned to the court of the Queen of England to answer why he should have 365 windows in his castle, the very same number as in the castle of her Royal Highness. With the use of his charm, Lord Louth apparently got away with having to block only one window.

Designs in the plasterwork mirror the pointed Gothic windows

Top floor room

Spiral staircase in
sixteenth-century tower

Side of house through
neo-Gothic window

Outbuildings to side of house

Hollymount House

Hollymount House was originally built in the early eighteenth century by John Vesey, Archbishop of Tuam. In 1668 Vesey had bought 750 acres in the barony of Kilmaine from the sale of the estate of Colonel John Browne of Westport. He went on to acquire another 2,000 acres from the sale of other forfeited estates.

In 1731 John Vesey sold part of his estate to his half-brother George Vesey, the rector of the village of Hollymount. George's daughter Frances married Thomas Lindsey in 1757 and they had one son, also Thomas Lindsey. This Thomas married Lady Margaret Eleanor Bingham, daughter of the first Earl of

A pile of rubble is all that remains of Hollymount House

Lucan. Hollymount was inherited by their first son, Thomas Spencer Lindsey. Thomas Spencer Lindsey was Justice of the Peace, Deputy Lieutenant and became High Sheriff in 1822.

In 1834 the architect George Papworth was employed to remodel the house. Papworth's other designs include St Mary's Pro-Cathedral, Dublin.

The front of the house was two storeys over basement and seven bays wide. The rear of the house was three storeys high and five bays wide. The severe front façade featured giant bold pilasters, with the entrance by a three-bay pedimented breakfront. The driveway to the house had massive gates which

Part of the vaulted basement survives beneath the rubble

Part of the basement kitchen still survives

featured vases and other carved figures. In later years it was said that these gates were sold off and re-erected at Kinsale, County Cork.

Thomas Spencer Lindsey also improved the Hollymount estate. The stables and farm buildings to the rear of the house were vastly expanded, several walled gardens were constructed and fruit and vegetable production benefited from the addition of heated greenhouses. Lindsey also had his own dairy, and the cheese produced on the estate was sent for sale in the markets of Yorkshire, where it was recognised as the finest of its kind.

Thomas Spencer Lindsey died in December 1867 and was succeeded by his second son, also named Thomas Spencer Lindsey. When he died in 1876, his daughter, Mary, inherited the estate which comprised 5,194 acres. Mary married Heremon FitzPatrick, grandson of the second Marquess of Headford and he took the additional surname of Lindsey. Mary died on 5 November 1895 and Heremon remarried, this time to Grace Agnes Malone on 25 July 1908.

In the 1911 census, the occupants are recorded as: Heremon Lindsey FitzPatrick, aged 51 and his wife Grace Agnes Lindsey FitzPatrick, aged 48. The house had a staff of eight: Hugh Melia, aged 35, footman; Frances Columan, aged 18, kitchen maid; Agnes Kinsella, aged 27, housemaid; Annie F. Canonon, aged 30, housemaid; Mary M. Brophy, aged 20, lady's maid; Mary Harker, aged 29, lady's maid; Mary Grogan, aged 29, cook; and William Fulham, aged 39, butler.

Extensive remains of outbuildings

View of yard behind house

Remains of greenhouse heating system

The Hollymount estate was sold to the Congested Districts Board on 31 March 1915. By 1931 the estate was in the possession of Mr McCartan and by 1940 the house and 56 acres became the property of Mr James Loftus. By 1948, Mr Loftus had died, and the house and lands were described as derelict and untenanted. Later the house would be totally demolished.

All that remains of the house today are a few scattered bricks and one corner of the old basement kitchen. The extensive stables, outbuildings and remains of the heated greenhouses hint at the prosperity of the nineteenth-century Hollymount estate.

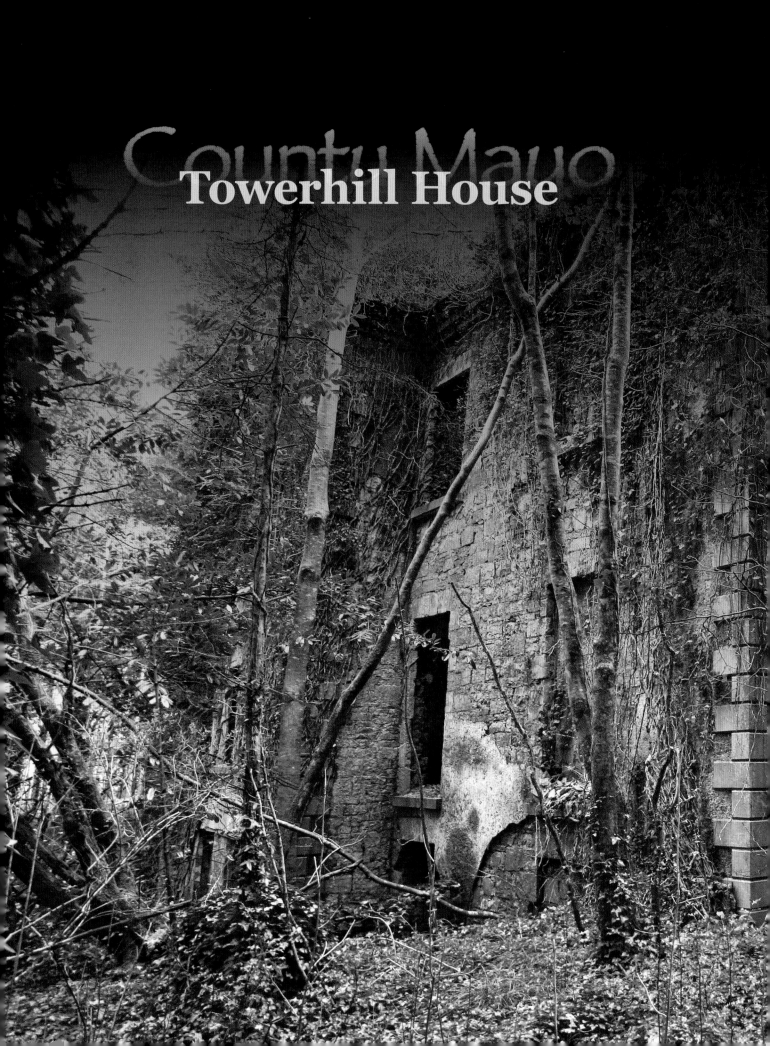

Towerhill House

Ivy-covered house interior

In 1766 Isidore Blake bought the lands of Towaghty, County Mayo, from Robert and Richard Blake of Ardfry. Towaghty became known as Towerhill and in 1790 Isidore built Towerhill House. The location chosen for the house was believed to be the site of an old burial place and church which had been dedicated to St Patrick. The house was a large mansion, two storeys over basement, six bays wide and three bays deep.

When Isidore Blake died, Towerhill was inherited by his son, Maurice Blake, a Deputy Lieutenant

View of back of house

Justice of the Peace and a major in the North Mayo Militia. When Maurice Blake died, he was succeeded by his son, Valentine O'Connor Blake.

In the spring of 1885 Valentine Blake reintroduced football into County Mayo. The first newspaper report of a match is dated 26 December 1885. The match was played at Towerhill on a Sunday, after the second Mass and lasted from 2.30 p.m. to 4.30 p.m. Ballyglass played Carnacon in a hard-fought battle, and after admiring the revival of the ancient national sport he provided a barrel from his cellar to provide refreshment for the players. The game went on to become hugely popular in the area and twelve months later Valentine's son Maurice was leading the Carnacon team in their green-and-red strip, the County Mayo colours. The Blakes provided a field for the Carnacon team which was known as 'The Bogey Field'. Soon after, however, the land agitation started and by 1909 most of the Blakes' estate had been sold off to the Congested Districts Board.

In the 1911 census, the occupants of the house are recorded as: Maurice C. F. Blake, aged 73, retired colonel; his wife, Jennette Blake, aged 69; daughter Olivia Blake, aged 45; son Valentine Blake, aged 44, retired captain; daughter Georgina Blake, aged 42; and daughter Margaret Blake, aged 36. The family had a staff of seven: Ellen Doogne, aged 24, domestic servant; Margaret Gaffrey, aged 62, domestic servant; Mary Higgins, aged 27, domestic servant; Sarah Bell, aged 27, domestic servant; Bridget Darmody, aged 85, dependant; Margaret Foy, aged 73, domestic servant and Michael Hayden, aged 28, servant butler.

Interior view showing blocked doorway and arched roof structure

Archway and scant remains of surviving plasterwork

243

Window with delicate remains of glazing

Front entrance hall interior with view through front door to surrounding forest

Wine cellar

Towerhill House was sold in the late 1940s and the Land Commission divided the estate between local farmers. Anything of use was taken from the house. Its roof was removed and the house abandoned.

Today the forest encroaches from all sides and Towerhill House is long forgotten. It is, however, still inhabited: the ruin offers ideal conditions for the hibernation of the Lesser Horseshoe bat. Up to fifty-six bats have been recorded at the house in recent years, making it a site of International Importance.

County Meath
Black Castle

Black Castle, built in 1760, was originally a single-storey gentleman's cottage with a thatched roof and large curved bows owned by the Fitzherbert family. John Ruxton married Letitia Fitzherbert and together they resided at the Black Castle cottage. Around 1791, with the help of the amateur architect Rev. Daniel Beaufort, John Ruxton added a slated two-storey wing to the rear of the house.

Black Castle was inherited by John's son, Richard, who, as a condition of his inheritance, assumed his mother's maiden name, becoming Richard Fitzherbert. In 1828 he replaced Black Castle cottage with

Side view of house showing remains of portico

a large two-storey, partially over basement mansion house. The house was six bays at the front, with the entrance through a Doric portico on a three-bay side. The opposite side of the house had a curved bow with a balcony on the upper floor and a further three-bay wing, which may have been the two-storey structure existing from the earlier house.

Richard died without children and the Black Castle estate was left to his aunt Mary's grandson, Thomas Rothwell, who also as a condition to his inheritance assumed the name Fitzherbert. Thomas died in 1879 and was succeeded by his son, Richard Fitzherbert.

House interior

Entrance hall leading to house interior

The rear of the house leads on to extensive outbuildings

250

Joy riders crashed a car into the portico and then set fire to the wreckage

At the time of the 1911 census, Richard was letting the house to Sir Francis Lee, who was visiting from England. Sir Francis states on the census form that he was in Ireland for a few weeks. He was accompanied by his wife, Alison, and a staff of eight including a secretary, butler, footman, cook, three maids and a nurse.

When Richard Fitzherbert died in 1920 the estate passed to his son, Bertram Fitzherbert. A tradition, which was maintained until Bertram's death, relates back to the Ruxton family who were said to still hold a claim to the property. On one day of the year, St Peter's Day, 29 June, any Ruxton entering the castle was entitled to stay on as owner of the property. To prevent any Ruxton accomplishing this, on every 29 June, all gates and entrances to Black Castle were locked and guarded. During the night, bonfires were lit and all the men of the area would stand guard whilst consuming wine and food supplied by the Fitzherberts.

Bertram died unmarried in 1939 and Black Castle was left to a relative, Ivo Fitzherbert, who went on to live in Argentina. Members of the Fitzherbert and Ruxton families are buried in a sarcophagus in Donaghmore church graveyard, in the shadow of the Donaghmore round tower.

The Black Castle estate operated as a farm and farm shop in the 1970s but eventually fell into disuse. The house was abandoned, and then fell victim to vandals, who eventually destroyed it by fire in 1987. Later joyriders crashed a car into the portico, the fallen columns of which still lie among the car wreck.

Black Castle has been the subject of two planning applications, the latest of which is for a hotel, eighteen townhouses and around 450 apartments.

County Meath
Dangan Castle

Dangan Castle first came into the possession of the Wesleys in the fourteenth century. When Garret Wesley died in 1728 the estate was left to his cousin Richard Colley on condition he assumed the name of Wesley. Richard Wesley was MP for Trim and in 1746 he was created Baron of Mornington. He set about improving the house and estate, spending vast sums on planting trees, laying out gardens and damming streams to form lakes and canals. Dangan Castle, initially a tower house, was rebuilt as a two-storey, five-bay mansion house.

View from south

In April 1733 Mrs Pendarves visited the house and recorded various activities in her memoirs: 'Breakfast was served at 10am, chocolate, tea, coffee, toast, butter, caudle etc are devoured without mercy. The hall is so large that very often breakfast, battledore, shuttlecock and harpsichord go on at the same time without molesting each other.'

Mrs Pendarves went on to describe the Dangan estate: 'Mr Wesley has three canals in his garden, in one he has the model of the King's yacht the Cumberland, the prettiest thing and it will hold two people

View from northwest

it has guns, colours, etc with as much exactness as the original. In another of his canals he has a barge which he calls the Pretty Betty, it will hold a dozen people and we are immediately going to try it. In the third canal he has a yawl, named Miss Fanny.'

The Dangan Castle gardens were more than 600 acres and contained at least twenty-five obelisks. Twenty-six acres of lakes had been constructed, with islands for wildfowl. At the edge of one of these lakes Wesley built a folly fort, complete with canons.

Wesley's first son, also named Richard, was born on 20 June 1760 and his second son, Arthur, was born on 1 May 1769. Arthur Wesley would go on to be granted a dukedom, becoming the Duke of Wellington, one of the most powerful men in Europe at that time.

By 1776 Richard Wesley's finances were dwindling: he had mortgaged his Kildare estates and owed more than £16,000 pounds. He moved his family to lodgings in Knightsbridge in London and sought various ways out of his financial predicament, even by purchasing lottery tickets. By May 1781 he was dead: some believed that the worry of his financial situation had been the end of him.

Plasterwork survives on the arch soffit

Outbuildings to rear of house

One of the surviving obelisks

The Wellington Monument was erected in the close-by town of Trim in 1817

House interior

On 18 September 1793 Dangan Castle was sold to Captain Thomas Burrowes of the 34th Cumberland Regiment for the sum of £25,000. It appears that Burrowes had no taste for water sports since he drained the canals and lakes and also converted much of the gardens to farmland. He lived at Dangan for a few years and then let the estate to Roger O'Connor of Connorville, County Cork (see p. 63). O'Connor had high notions and saw himself entertaining Emperor Napoleon at Dangan Castle. O'Connor's brother, Arthur, had moved to France in 1803 and been appointed an honorary General by Napoleon. In a strange quirk of fate, Arthur Wesley, the aforementioned Duke of Wellington, defeated Napoleon on Sunday 18 June 1815 at the Battle of Waterloo.

O'Connor was a very bad tenant not only in paying rent, but also in preserving the property. The Dangan estate was stripped of its trees and turned into a shabby wreck. Dangan Castle was gutted of its valuable materials and in 1809 a fire left it devastated. The O'Connors returned to Cork, leaving Dangan Castle an abandoned burnt-out ruin.

By 1827 Arthur Wesley, Duke of Wellington, was at the forefront of European society and Dangan Castle, his supposed birthplace, became a tourist attraction. A Mr Peter Allen made a few rooms of the ruin habitable and lived there with his family. For a small payment, Allen would show any curious visitor the very spot where the Duke of Wellington had first come into this world.

Today Dangan Castle is little more than a tumbledown ruin. Nothing remains of the previously magnificent lakes and canals. One obelisk stands on a distant hill as a testament to what was once amongst the finest demesnes in Ireland.

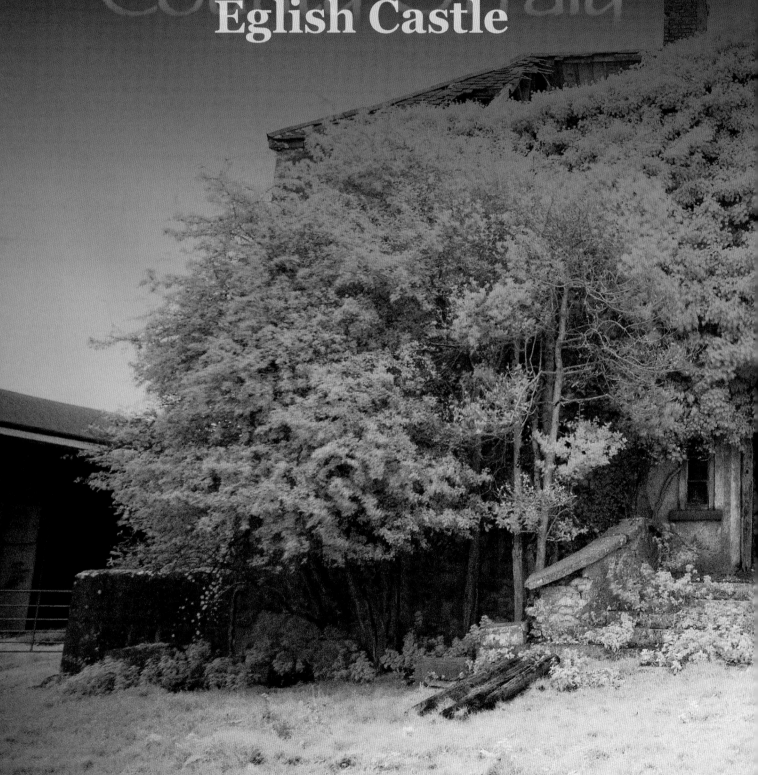

County Offaly

Eglish Castle

Eglish Castle, built by the O'Molloys, was originally the strongest castle in the area and gave its name to the barony of Eglish.

By 1760 Eglish Castle was occupied by the Berry family and when Knight Berry married Sophia Stirling, her dowry paid for the castle to be rebuilt as a mansion house with parts of the old castle walls being incorporated into the eastern side of the house.

An interesting story relates to Mr Berry, then the owner of Eglish Castle, and his neighbour, John

360° view of front entrance hall (It appears to have been more recently used as a bedroom)

O'Molloy, a descendant of the O'Molloys who built the original castle. John O'Molloy always considered himself of the highest nobility and wore a three-cocked hat and carried a long curved sword at his waist. One day when O'Molloy was amusing himself by cutting the heads off thistles with his sword, he was approached by Mr Berry who thought the eccentric-looking Molloy to be some kind of lunatic.

Mr Berry enquired with contempt, 'Who are you, Sir?'

O'Molloy replied, 'The Chief.'

▲ Steps leading to front door

View from basement to collapsed
rear structure of house ▶

'My name's Berry', was returned, to
which O'Molloy replied, 'And, I believe, a
bitter berry too.'

According to onlookers Mr Berry was
fortunate that it was only the heads of thistles
that were chopped off with O'Molloy's sword.

In 1837 Eglish Castle was the residence
of Captain English. The 1911 census records
the occupants of the castle as: Frederick
Dillon, aged 60, gentleman farmer; his two
daughters Aileen K. Dillon, aged 21, and Lily
E. G. Dillon, aged 17; and his son Frederick
W. Dillon, aged 14. The Dillons had one
domestic servant: Norah Tarleton, aged 18.
At the time of the census Frederick's wife,
Elizabeth, was not present in the house.

Today Eglish Castle is slowly crumbling.
Plasterwork clings to leaking ceilings,
floorboards are rotten and failing and much
of the interior structure has collapsed.

▲ Debris-covered corridor with remains of bicycle on floor

▲ Mirror with wine glasses left on mantlepiece

▼ Remains of staircase with baluster left on first floor landing

Geashill Castle

Archway with some surviving moulding leading to front door

The first Geashill Castle was built by the FitzGeralds around the year 1203. It was a fortress three storeys high with a spiral stairway leading to the top, where there was purportedly an iron chair. An underground passage ran to the adjoining abbey. In 1307 the O'Connors attacked and destroyed Geashill, and in the same year the fifth Baron of Offaly John Fitz Thomas rebuilt it.

Around 1406 Geashill was again attacked. According to tradition the attacking armies had a great cauldron in which beer was brewed. The cauldron was being carried on the back of one of the young attackers. Calvagh O'Conor had a stone in his hand and, taking a chance, he threw it at the invaders. The stone struck the cauldron and produced such an unearthly noise that sudden terror and panic were struck

View of rear ground floor

into the hearts of the invaders and they instantly fled. They were pursued into the bog north of Geashill town and surrounded; more than 300 of the invading men were slain. The beer cauldron was lost to the bog but would resurface some 400 years later.

In 1599 when William FitzGerald, thirteenth Earl of Kildare, was returning from England, his ship was battered by a storm and sank; all on board drowned, leaving his niece Lettice FitzGerald as the heir to Geashill Castle. Lettice married Robert Digby of Warwickshire, England. Digby was knighted in 1596, and became MP for Athy in 1613. He died on 24 May 1618 and was buried in the church of Coleshill in Warwickshire, leaving his wife Lettice Digby, Lady Offaly, as head of the house at Geashill.

When the rebellion of 1641 broke out, Lady Offaly, then aged 62, was residing at Geashill. The castle came under attack by an army led by her cousin Henry O'Dempsey. A series of letters was exchanged between the invading O'Dempsey and the defending Lady Offaly, but it achieved nothing. The O'Dempseys summoned a blacksmith who collected all pots and pans in the locality and smelted the iron to produce a cannon. The next day the weapon was brought forward and directed towards the castle. However, on the first discharge the cannon burst, much to the amusement of Lady Offaly's garrison. A barrage of musket fire broke out, whereupon a bullet happened to strike the wall near Lady Offaly; she immediately wiped the spot with her handkerchief, showing just what she thought of the enemy's attack. Some days later a force rode out of Dublin and came to the Lady Offaly's rescue. She continued residence at the castle for several months before again being threatened by the O'Dempseys. This time she retired to her late husband's family home in Warwickshire where she died in 1658, aged 79.

Geashill remained in the hands of the Digbys. Lady Offaly's descendants rebuilt Geashill Castle into a comfortable mansion house, seven bays at the front with a recessed three-bay centre. By 1837 the Digby estate was the largest in County Offaly, consisting of 34,000 acres. The ninth Baron, Lord Digby, carried out extensive improvements in the 1860s and 1870s resulting in the village of Geashill being recorded as the neatest, cleanest and best kept in all of Ireland.

Lord Digby would, however, be caught up in a legal battle in which the legitimate claim to his estates was challenged, his tenants' rights over lands were questioned and around fifty families were evicted.

Crumbling house interior

View of second floor archway

In the 1911 census the occupants of Geashill castle are recorded as: Regneald Digby, aged 63; his wife, Caroleus Grace Digby, aged 59; and two daughters: Edith Digby, aged 33 and Maud Digby, aged 30. The Digby family had a staff of five: Jane Farrell, aged 29, cook; Mary Margret Reenan, aged 26, parlour maid; Alice Kelly, aged 33, housemaid; Annie Coupar, aged 24, maid; and Kathleen Dunne, aged 19, kitchen maid.

By this time the beer cauldron had reappeared. It was discovered in a bog and displayed by Regneald Digby in his mansion. It was described as a huge hammered copper cauldron about 3 feet 8 inches in diameter. Geashill Castle was reputed to be badly haunted, the manifestations of which were associated with the ancient cauldron.

In 1922, during the Irish Civil War, Geashill Castle was set on fire and burnt to the ground. Today, just its walls remain, standing as an impressive, romantic ruin.

County Roscommon
Rockingham Demesne

Rockingham House

Rockingham Demesne

In the tenth century a deal was made between two brothers of the MacDermot clan, the younger brother giving up his claims to the lordship of Connacht in exchange for the lands around Lough Key. The area went on to become known as Moylurg and became a stronghold of the MacDermots until they were displaced by Cromwell in 1649.

One of Cromwell's soldiers, Sir John King, was granted lands around Boyle Abbey. Later the King family would become amongst the most powerful in Ireland. Successive members of the King family built a series of mansion houses close to Lough Key, on the Rockingham Demesne. The largest of these mansion houses was Rockingham House, construction of which was started in 1810. General Robert King, who became first Viscount Lorton commissioned John Nash, one of the finest architects of country houses of the time, to design the house. John Nash went on to design much of Regency London, including Trafalgar Square and Buckingham Palace.

When Rockingham House was complete Viscount Lorton went on to construct a number of follies in the Rockingham Demesne including gatehouses, the estate chapel, the Fairy Bridge and Cloontykilla Castle. He also transformed the old MacDermot castle on Castle Island into a folly castle. Rockingham House and demesne became one of the finest estates in Ireland.

At 7 p.m. on 10 September 1957 disaster struck when a footman discovered a fire in the basement of the house. The fire soon ran out of control and, despite the efforts of every available fire engine and fireman in the area, Rockingham House was completely gutted. Sir Cecil Stafford King-Harmon, then the owner of Rockingham, considered rebuilding the house but did not have the resources to engage in such an expensive project. He bought St Catherines Park in Leixlip, County Kildare, which later became the Liffey Valley House Hotel.

In 1959 the Rockingham Demesne was offered at public auction, taken over by the Land Commission and the estate divided amongst local farmers. The massive ruined shell of Rockingham House stood for the next fourteen years. In 1971 the Irish State made the strange decision to demolish the house and replace it with an ugly reinforced-concrete viewing tower which looks out over Lough Key.

Rockingham Gatehouse

The Gatehouse is one of the finest features still standing in the Rockingham Demesne. In its present condition however it is unclear as to just how long it will remain standing.

Rockingham Gatehouse

View of first floor with internal structure collapsing

Unstable staircase to first floor

Castle Island, Rockingham Demesne

Tomaltach 'of the Rock' is credited with building the first stone castle on Castle Island around the year 1200. The Rock became the headquarters of the MacDermot clan and their fortress a renowned centre of hospitality; it was said any person calling on them would receive food and shelter no matter what their social standing. According to legend, when Una Bhan MacDermot fell deeply in love with a member of a rival family – Thomas Laidir McCostello – her father confined her to Castle Island where she died of a broken heart. McCostello would secretly swim out every night to visit her grave. Finally the cold waters were the end of McCostello and the two were reunited when his grave was placed next to hers. It is said two rose trees grew over their graves and became entwined in a lover's knot.

Castle Island is located a short distance from the Lough Key shoreline

View of castle from west

View of castle interior

Eastern castle balcony

After Cromwell passed through, the island was abandoned and the castle left to decay. In the 1830s Viscount Lorton rebuilt the castle, transforming it into a folly.

William Butler Yeats visited the island on 13 May 1890, and was so transfixed by it that he planned on turning the island into a place 'where a mystical order would retire for a while for contemplation'. His idea came to nothing.

Castle rear entrance

View through Gothic window to castle interior

Cloontykilla Castle, Rockingham Demesne

In 1839, Cloontykilla Castle was built on the Rockingham Demesne for use as a hunting and fishing lodge. The castle has four towers, one with a spiral staircase leading to the top. The courtyard contains a five-bay, two-storey house, of which the top floor windows are 'blind' with fireplaces built in the walls directly behind.

Cloontykilla Castle served as the Irish Republican Brotherhood's western command centre and was used for planning the Easter Rising of 1916. The castle was used throughout the War of Independence and when the hostilities ended a large cache of arms was discovered.

In 2004 Cloontykilla Castle was for sale for €950,000. Today it is undergoing restoration and conversion into a modern comfortable residence.

View through entrance archway to castle courtyard (the date 1839 is carved in the arch keystone)

Courtyard interior

View from top of tower

The rear of the castle is finished with Gothic windows, the lower of which are blind

County Sligo
Seafield House

The Phibbs family originated in England: two brothers, William and Richard, both soldiers, arrived in Ireland around 1590. William settled in Cork and Richard, who received a pension as a maimed soldier in 1619, settled in Dublin. William's descendants went on to build up substantial landholdings in Sligo, Roscommon and Westmeath.

The Phibbs family acquired the Seafield estate in County Sligo late in the eighteenth century and the first Seafield House was built by Owen Phibbs in 1798.

In 1840 Owen's son, William Phibbs, commissioned the architect John Benson to build him a new mansion house on the Seafield estate. The contract for building was awarded to the Dublin builder Arthur

360° view of house interior

Murray; the cost of construction was £4,200 with an additional £1,400 paid for plumbing, decorating and the erection of a windmill which acted as a water pump. The architect John Benson went on to be knighted for his design of the Dublin Exhibition building of 1853.

The new Seafield House was built to classical design, square in plan with two storeys and an entrance front of seven bays. The recessed doorway was flanked by two Ionic columns. The garden side of the house was five bays with the centre three bays recessed and extending with a cast iron veranda. The interior of the house featured a large hall, ballroom and library. The second floor held a large gallery lit by skylights.

It is said that William's first son, Owen (grandson of the Owen Phibbs who built Seafield House)

Window with fine moulded architrave and pediment

Window console

travelled through the Far East, Syria and Egypt, returning to Ireland with a booty of ancient treasures. These objects were installed in the first floor gallery room, which became known as 'the museum'. Trouble started soon afterwards when the house became infested with a particularly unpleasant poltergeist. The house was handed over to a group of Jesuit priests who performed Mass daily for some weeks in an attempt to exorcise the poltergeist. One of the priests involved in the exorcism, Father Stephen Brown, went on to work in the British Museum, the Bodleian and various other libraries. In an attempt to shake its haunted reputation Seafield House was renamed Lisheen House. The tale of the poltergeist may, however, just be a popular myth. Mrs Rawlin, aged 95, the granddaughter of Owen Phibbs, has no knowledge of any paranormal events occurring at Lisheen House.

Owen Phibbs inherited the estate and is recorded in the 1911 census: Owen Phibbs, aged 70, landed proprietor. He had a staff of five: Mary Barbara Rogers, aged 50, cook; Issabelle Collins, aged 26, parlour maid; Emily Frances Hicks, aged 23, housemaid; Margaret McGloin, aged 21, kitchen maid; and Elizabeth Magee, aged 30, laundress.

Owen Phibbs died in 1914 and was succeeded by his son Basil. Basil's son, Geoffrey, wrote that his father had once fired a shot at soldiers of the Irish Republican Army who were attempting invasion of Lisheen House across the tennis court. Basil apparently widely missed his target. According to popular belief, his aim was no better when it came to pheasants.

Basil was not pleased at his son's choice of wife, Norah McGuinness, whom Geoffrey married in 1924. Norah was forbidden entry into Lisheen House and in protest Geoffrey changed his surname to his mother's maiden name, becoming Geoffrey Ingram Taylor.

Geoffrey was considered to be the black sheep of the family: he wore inappropriate clothing and had long hair. However, he achieved some success as a poet, writer and editor. He separated from Norah when he moved to London and entered into a *ménage à quatre* in 1929 with the poets Robert Graves, Laura Riding and Graves' wife, Nancy. After the *quatre* separated, Geoffrey lived with Nancy.

Around 1940 Lisheen House was sold by Geoffrey's brother, Denis William Phibbs, to Isaac Beckett of Ballina, County Mayo, for £1,400. Beckett later sold the house. It was stripped of its contents, the roof removed and the house abandoned.

Ground floor front room

House interior

Loughmoe Court was the seat of the Purcell family, Barons of Loughmoe. In 1171, during the Anglo-Norman invasion, Sir Hugh Purcell had come to Ireland with Strongbow. Purcell did not get far; he was slain at Waterford. His death was recorded by Giraldus Cambrensis thus: 'on the morrow, seeking to cross the river in one of the native boats to hold parley with the King, the boatmen rose upon him in the middle of the stream, stabbed him with their long skeans and then threw the body into the river.'

Sir Hugh Purcell left two sons and in 1204 his first son, also named Hugh, married Beatrix, daughter of Theobald FitzWalter, Chief Butler of Ireland. In the marriage settlement, he received the lands of Loughmoe. According to legend, FitzWalter wished to rid the countryside of vicious beasts and as no

House interior with entrance to tower at the rear

hunter had yet managed to accomplish this, he offered a prize: the lands of Loughmoe and also his daughter's hand in marriage. Accepting this challenge, young Purcell made his way through the forest by leaping from branch to branch until eventually he came across the savage creatures below him. With his bow, he let free an onslaught of arrows until two shots went into the mouths of the beasts and they ran in pain and terror. They were later found dead near Thurles. Hugh Purcell claimed his prize, through which Loughmoe derives its name (in Irish *'Luach Mhagh'*, meaning 'The field of the reward').

In 1328 Richard Purcell was granted the title Baron of Loughmoe and the Purcell family would continue to prosper for the next few centuries.

Loughmoe Court was originally a fifteenth-century tower house, five storeys high with the first and top floor vaulted. The principal chamber was a fine room some 37 feet long by 29 feet wide. The top floor is said to hold a secret prison chamber.

In the seventeenth century, the Purcells went on to expand Loughmoe Court dramatically by the addition of a semi-fortified mansion house. The new structure was a three-storey-over-basement wing attached to the old tower house, with a square tower at the opposite end to add balance. The mansion featured huge mullioned windows and fine fireplaces which can still be seen in the outer walls. The most ornate fireplace was added into the old tower house and has the arms of the Purcells and Butlers engraved into its mantle.

Spiral staircase in tower viewed through pointed door arch

View of house wall to fifteenth-century tower

View of house interior from top of tower

Another legend surrounding Loughmoe Court is in regard to the adjoining, remarkably flat and level grass field. It is said that one of the Loughmoe barons was so fond of the game of hurley that he kept his own private team of hurlers. The finest hurler in the area, a man named Londergan, had the strength of an ox and the speed of an Arabian stallion. Using his hurley, he could strike a ball so high over Loughmoe Court that he could run to the far side of the castle and strike the ball again on its descent. His record stood at performing this feat nine times in succession before the ball fell to the ground.

During the 1641 Rebellion, Theobald Purcell took the side of the Confederate Catholics. Loughmoe Court was attacked and recorded as destroyed and 'out of all manner of repayre'. The Purcells, however, continued occupying the castle. The last Baron of Loughmoe, Nicholas Purcell, fought at the Battle of the Boyne and was a signatory to the Treaty of Limerick. In 1705 he became one of the few Catholics to be given the authority to carry weapons: one sword, one case of pistols and one gun. Nicholas Purcell's son had a gruesome end: he fell into a vat of boiling water and died, leaving Nicholas' daughter to inherit Loughmoe Court. She married a young man named White from Leixlip, County Kildare. At the time of their marriage White was still a boy. The young Purcell lady refused to live with him until he was eighteen years old.

The Purcell-Whites were the last to live in Loughmoe Court; they abandoned the castle around 1760.

Stone fireplaces in the eastern wall
of the house

View through arch to fine fireplace
located in first floor of tower

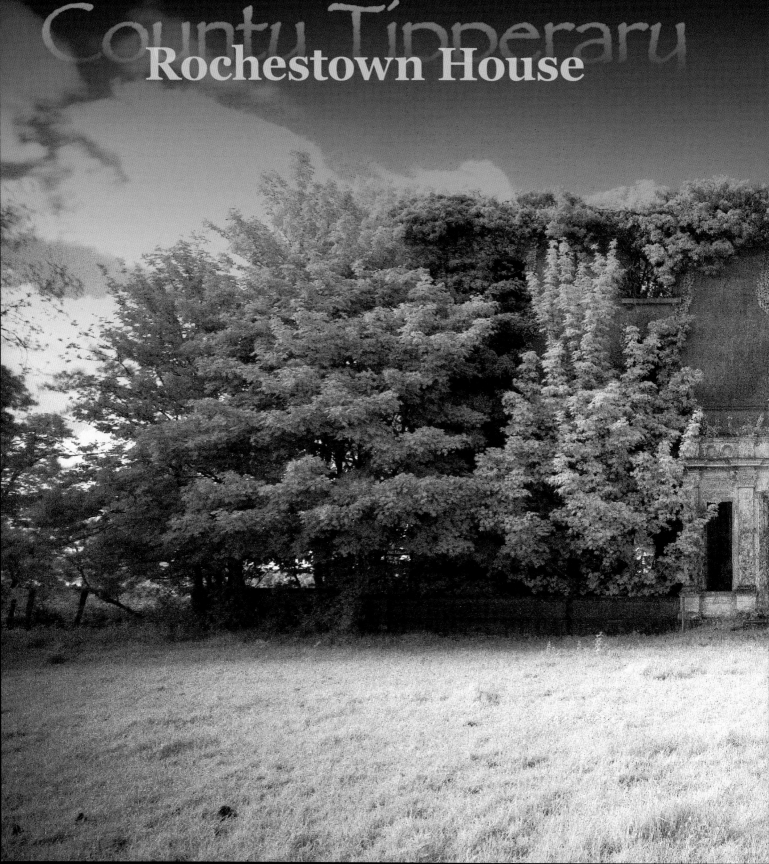

County Tipperary
Rochestown House

Rochestown House began as a Georgian mansion house, built by Dunbar Barton in the 1820s. Dunbar's grandfather Thomas Barton had emigrated to Bordeaux, earning the nickname 'French Tom'. In 1725 he formed a shipping company, eventually becoming the largest exporter of wine in all of France, even shipping to Thomas Jefferson, the third president of the United States. At that time Bordeaux wine was recognised as the very finest and its largest market was amongst the gentlemen and aristocracy of Ireland. Over the next decades the Barton family became extremely wealthy.

Interior of front porch

The winemaker Barton and Guestier, formed by Dunbar's brother Hugh Barton and Daniel Guestier, is still one of the most successful French wine distributors today. Ronald Barton remained as the head of the company until 1986. Today it is owned by Diageo.

Dunbar Barton married Elizabeth Riall in 1798. When his wife inherited the Rochestown estate they set about building a mansion house. The house was of Georgian design, attributed to the architect Sir Richard Morrison. It was two storeys over basement, five bays at the front with a three-bay breakfront and an Ionic doorway with a fanlight.

Very fine front entrance porch ▲

Carved sandstone in front porch ▶

The artist Rose Maynard Barton, daughter of Dunbar's third son, Augustine Barton, was born at Rochestown in 1858; Rose went on to exhibit at the Royal Hibernian Academy, the Royal Academy and the Grosvenor Gallery in London. Her watercolours and townscapes of Tipperary, Dublin and London are highly respected and held in many collections in England and Ireland.

Dunbar Barton was succeeded at Rochestown by his son Samuel Barton, and Samuel by his son, Colonel Christopher Barton. Christopher sold the house in the mid-1860s. The new owners, the Wise family, commissioned the architect Sir Thomas Newenham Deane to remodel Rochestown House.

Sir Thomas Deane's Gothic-influenced designs included the museum at Trinity College and the Kildare Street Club, Dublin. He went on to become the first Inspector of National Monuments of Ireland under the Irish Board of Works after the Church of Ireland lost control of the nation's heritage monuments.

Fine cut-stone balcony and bay window

Interior of bowed wing

The house is surrounded by a moat, allowing light and access to the basement

The new Rochestown House was complete in 1867 and was unrecognisable from the original house. A third storey, an extravagant porch and a sweeping wing were added and the entire structure was finished with a fine Italianate facade. After these works Rochestown House rated amongst the most magnificent in Tipperary. In 1871 Charles W. Wise is listed as owning 322 acres at Rochestown. He settled down at Rochestown and became a very successful horse breeder. He was succeeded by his son, Major Francis Herbert Wise.

The 1911 census records the occupants as: Francis Wise, aged 42, retired lieutenant major; his wife, Jane Wise, aged 41; son William Wise, aged 12; daughter Beatrice Wise, aged 6; and son Brendon Wise, aged 3. The Wise family had a staff of seven: Kate Kenny, aged 23, parlour maid; Anny Jones, aged 44, nurse; Bridget Voss, aged 22, housemaid; Bridget Cahill, aged 23, nursery maid; Ann Whitty, aged 25, housemaid; Ann Frost, aged 44, cook; and Kate Chanoher, aged 21, kitchen maid. Mrs Wise's sister, Agnes Little, aged 42, also resided at the Rochestown.

On the morning of 18 November 1918 a fire broke out in the house. Mrs Wise, her children and her sister all escaped unhurt. The building was not too badly damaged but much of the furniture was destroyed. During the Irish Civil War, on 17 February 1923, a second fire was deliberately started and this time Rochestown was burnt to the ground, leaving it uninhabitable.

The Wise family built a new house on the estate where they continued to operate a successful horse stud. Today the empty ruin of Rochestown House is slowly being covered by undergrowth and the fine cut-stone walls and Italianate balconies are disappearing behind nettles and ivy.

County Westmeath
Ballynagall House

Ballynagall derives its name from the Anglo-Norman invaders. Hugh de Lacy had obtained thousands of acres in Westmeath and gave the lands of *Baile na nGall* or 'The Town of the Foreigners' to his followers. In 1720 Colonel Arthur Reynell bought the lands and built Castle Reynell. In 1803 Castle Reynell was bought by James Gibson and in 1808 James' son, also named James, commissioned the architect Francis Johnston to build a new mansion house. Ballynagall was built over the old Castle Reynall at a cost of over £30,000. When complete it was described as a splendid mansion and one of the finest and most extensively planted demesnes in the country.

360° view of the kitchen which stands in a wing attached to the north end of the house. The fireplace and turreted chimney appear to date from the earlier Castle Reynell structure

The house was two storeys over basement, six bays at the front with a single storey Ionic portico and single storey, two-bay wings. The entrance led into a hall, to the right was a drawing room with pink walls and green and gold mouldings, the drawing room led through to a Richard Turner conservatory which looked out over the gardens. The dining room was green with gold decorations, had red curtains and housed a dining table that could seat thirty-six. The ground floor contained many other reception rooms including a billiard room and smoking room. The staircase, also designed by Francis Johnston, ran the full height of the house and had brass banisters and a mahogany handrail. The second floor contained numerous bedchambers, containing four-poster beds.

When James Gibson died, he left Ballynagall to his nephew by marriage, James Middleton Berry. Berry left the house to his cousin Thomas Smyth.

The 1911 census records the occupants of Ballynagall as: Thomas James Smyth, aged 77, Justice of the Peace; his son Hawkesworth Smyth, aged 45, Captain East York Regiment (retired on pay); Hawkesworth's wife, Constance Smyth, aged 38; and their daughter, Gwendoline Smyth, aged 1. The Smyth family had a staff of nine: Jane Edwards, aged 48, nurse; Elizabeth Kerr, aged 33, cook; Jane Watkins, aged 27, housemaid; Ethel Hunt, aged 21, housemaid; Mary Hetherstone, aged 20, kitchen maid; Nellie L'Estrange, aged 19, kitchen maid; Sarah Allingham, aged 40, parlour maid; Louisa Young, aged 23, parlour maid; and Julia Heary, aged 19, nurse maid.

Most of the interior structure has collapsed; here the vaulted basement ceiling has also given way

View of debris-filled porch

This window lit the Francis Johnston-designed staircase, of which almost nothing remains

In 1962 Major Thomas Smyth sold Ballynagall to Mr Cronin and Mr MacDonald. The house was again sold in 1971. In 1981 Ballynagall House was dismantled; anything of use was removed and the house left as a roofless shell. The fine portico found a new home at the entrance to the K Club, Straffan, County Kildare, and the Turner conservatory at the La Serre restaurant on the Lyons estate, Celbridge, County Kildare.

The vast basement corridor still stands in reasonable condition at the centre of the ruin

The Ballynagall portico found a new home at the K Club, Straffan House, County Kildare. (photograph courtesy of Jessica Collins)

The Ballynagall conservatory found a new home at the La Serre Restaurant on the Lyons estate, Celbridge, County Kildare. (photograph courtesy of Jessica Collins)

In 1740 Robert Rochfort, Lord Bellfield and later first Earl of Belvedere, commissioned the architect Richard Castle to build him a hunting lodge. At that time Richard Castle was recognised as the greatest architect in Ireland. Belvedere was built as a two-storey-over-basement, five-bay Palladian villa. Despite its appearance, the house contained very few rooms; they were, however, well proportioned and featured extremely fine rococo plasterwork on the ceilings.

Robert's family home was Gaulston House, also in County Westmeath, and he intended to use Belvedere as a retreat. But shortly after the house was complete, Robert accused his wife, Mary Molesworth, of committing adultery with his younger brother, Arthur Rochfort, who lived close by in Bellfield House. As punishment he put her under house arrest in Gaulston House while he moved permanently to Belvedere. She spent the next thirty-one years forbidden to see anybody other than servants, creating one of the greatest social scandals of eighteenth-century Ireland.

Robert's brother Arthur was dispossessed, sued for £2,000 and he died destitute in a debtors' prison. Robert's other brother George Rochfort also commissioned Richard Castle to build him a mansion

The Jealous Wall

Rochfort House (which later became known as Tudenham House, see p. 316) was built next door to Belvedere and was a far larger and superior house.

Robert, who was consumed with anger and jealousy over his brother's fine mansion, had a wall built between the two houses, blocking his view of his brother's residence. This wall, the largest folly ever built in Ireland, standing three storeys high and over 180 feet long, became known as 'The Jealous Wall'.

By the time Robert Rochfort died in 1744 he had acquired the nickname 'The Wicked Earl' and it was said he was murdered for all his wicked deeds. When his wife was finally released from captivity, old and haggard, she fled to France, became a nun and spent the remainder of her life as a hermit.

No children were ever born at Belvedere. The house was passed from cousin to cousin: Charles Kenneth Howard-Bury owned it in 1912 and from Charles it was handed to Rex Beaumont in 1963. In 1982 Westmeath County Council bought the estate for £250,000, the house was restored and is now open to the public.

Tudenham House

Tudenham House, built by George Rochfort in 1742, was first called Rochfort House. Rochfort employed the architect Richard Castle, who had also designed George's brother's house next door; Belvedere House (see p. 312).

Rochfort House was a very fine three-storey house, seven bays at the front with a central niche and oculus and seven bays on each of the sides which featured central curved bows. The front doorway led into a great hall with columns at both ends. Four large reception rooms with fine plasterwork, a library, billiard room and gun room were accessed from the hall. The two-storey upper hall had a large dome which was

View of house from west

reglazed with stained glass in the nineteenth century. Eight bedrooms and a bathroom were found on the first floor and the top floor held a further suite of bedrooms. The vaulted basement was immense, with a huge kitchen and the servants' quarters. The Rochfort estate amounted to over 850 acres.

Rochfort House was sold in the Landed Estates Court in 1836 and bought by Sir Francis Hopkins, second Baronet of Athboy. Sir Francis renamed the property Tudenham House. He died in 1860 and left the house to his sister, Anna Maria, who was married to Nicholas Loftus Tottenham. Anna Maria built a new front lodge to the house, and moved the driveway, making it exactly one mile long.

View from doorway looking up to first and second floors

Doric front entrance

The 1911 census records the occupants of Tudenham as: Charles Gore Loftus Tottenham, aged 49; his wife, Georgina Alice Lizzie Tottenham, aged 48; and their two daughters, Dorothea Loftus Tottenham, aged 20, and Angela Frances Deans Loftus Tottenham, aged 9. Charles' first son, Harold William Loftus Tottenham, had by then moved to South Africa. The Tottenhams had seven servants living in the house: a governess, a general maid, two housemaids, a cook, kitchen maid and footman. They also employed a laundress, a groom, a gamekeeper, coachman, chauffeur, butler and two gardeners, who lived in various cottages on the Tudenham demesne.

Stairway with surviving plasterwork

Fine plasterwork survives in the arch soffits

Vaulted kitchen with magnificent fireplace

During the First World War the house was used as a hospital. Charles Tottenham died in 1929 leaving his wife, Georgina, as the head of the household. Charles's son Harold returned from South Africa and occupied Tudenham for some years but the enormous house was very difficult to maintain. Harold extended the garden cottage and made it into a comfortable family home.

During the Second World War the house was occupied by the Irish Army. After the war the house was unused. Eventually in 1957 anything of use was removed; doors, wall coverings, fireplaces and furniture all found new homes. The roof was removed and the house left as an empty shell. The Tudenham estate was taken over by the Land Commission, which divided it into five farms, which were then let to various tenants.

Basement corridor

County Wexford
Castleboro House

Around 1628 Robert Carew obtained a grant of lands in County Wexford which had formerly belonged to the Desmonds. In 1668 Charles II confirmed the lands to Robert Carew's son, also named Robert, whereon he built a fortress known as Bally Boro Castle. The Carew first-born sons would continue to be named Robert for the next few centuries, creating something of a genealogical headache.

Towards the end of the eighteenth century Robert Carew wished to build a more modern residence; however, since he did not wish to commit to the expense of such a construction without an heir, the mansion was only started on the day his son Robert Shapland Carew was born, 9 March 1787. The new

360° view of house interior

mansion house was renamed Castleboro. Robert Shapland Carew became the first Baron Carew in the Peerage of Ireland in 1834 and also Baron Carew of Castle Boro in the Peerage of the United Kingdom in 1838.

In 1840, when the Carews were away, one of the chimneys caught fire and flames quickly spread through the whole house. Only the west wing was left standing. Lord Carew commissioned the architect Daniel Robertson to design a new mansion house. Robertson had built many other country houses in Classical and Gothic Revival style, including Johnstown Castle and Wilton Castle, both also in County

Ionic columns on the west wing

Wexford. It is said Robertson suffered from gout and spent much of his time at Castleboro being pushed around in a wheelbarrow, the plans for the house in one hand and a bottle of wine in the other.

Castleboro House was completed in 1848 at a cost of £84,000, in those days an enormous sum. The house was built in the Palladian style; a main central block, three storeys over basement, seven bays at the front and six bays at the side, with matching three-bay, two-storey pavilions joined by three-bay, two-storey corridors. The interior of the house featured a vast two-storey hall with a gallery, a suite of drawing rooms, a two-storey library and numerous other reception rooms. The grounds were laid out with four stepped terraces leading down to an artificial lake and were deemed to be second only to Powerscourt, County Wicklow. Trees were planted throughout the grounds by a number of notable visitors including the Duke of Clarence, the Prince of Wales, the Duke of Aosta, the Count of Turin and the Earl of Halsbury. Queen Victoria is reputed to have made many visits to the house and on one occasion played piano and sang to the Carew children.

View of house from southwest

View of garden entrance

View from basement level looking upwards

After the death of the first Baron Carew, the family spent a lot of time away from the house. The 1911 census records the occupants as just: Rosina Jane Baker, aged 40 head housemaid; Margaret Telford, aged 29, second housemaid; and Louisa Mary Greene, aged 20, under housemaid. The Castleboro demesne was also staffed by a dairy maid, three gardeners, a gamekeeper and numerous labourers.

In 1919 the Carew family, anticipating the War of Independence, left for England. They took most of their belongings and effects with them and left the house furnished only for occasional visits.

On the night of Monday 5 February 1923 Irish Republican Army irregulars soaked hay in paraffin and dragged the flaming bales through the house; the mansion burnt to the ground. Lord Carew died in London just two months later.

The current and seventh Baron Carew, Patrick Connolly-Carew, represented Ireland in the 1972 Olympics for the equestrian three-day event.

The main block of the house is surrounded by a broad moat, giving light and allowing access to the vast basement

View of house interior

Bibliography

Books

Adams, C. L., *Castles of Ireland* (London, 1904)

Anderson, J., *A Genealogical History of the House of Yvery* (London, 1742)

Bary, Valerie, *Historical, Genealogical and Architectural notes of some Houses of Kerry* (Whitegate, 1994)

Bence-Jones, Mark, *A Guide to Irish Country Houses* (London, 1988)

Blake, Martin J., *Blake Family Records 1600–1700* (London, 1902)

Brewer, J. N., *The Beauties of Ireland* (London, 1826)

Burke, Sir Bernard, *A Genealogical and Heraldic Dictionary of the Landed Gentry of Great Britain and Ireland* (London, 1871)

— *A Genealogical and Heraldic Dictionary of the Landed Gentry of Ireland* (London, 1912)

— *A Genealogical History of the Dormant, Abeyant, Forfeited and Extinct Peerages of the British Empire* (London, 1883)

— *A Second Series of Vicissitudes of Families and Other Essays* (London, 1861)

— *Family Romance or Episodes in the Domestic Annals of the Aristocracy* (London, 1854)

— *Rise of Great Families, other essays and stories* (London, 1873)

— *The General Armoury of England, Scotland, Wales; Comprising A Registry of Armorial Bearings From the Earliest To the Present Time* (London, 1884)

— *Vicissitudes of Families* (London, 1860)

Carrigan, Rev. William, *History and Antiquities of the Diocese of Ossory* (Dublin, 1905)

Clapison, John & Mullaney-Dignam, Triona, *Rockingham, Memories of a Vanished Mansion* (Boyle, 2007)

Craig, Maurice, *Classic Irish Houses of the Middle Size* (London, 1976)

Dutton, Hely, *Statistical and Agricultural Survey of the County of Galway* (Dublin, 1824)

Gibson, Rev. C. B., *The History of the County and City of Cork* (London, 1861)

Griffith, Sir Richard, *Griffith's Valuation of Ireland* (Dublin, 1848–1864)

Harbison, Peter, *Guide to National and Historic Monuments of Ireland* (Dublin, 2001)

Howard, Joseph Jackson & Crisp, Frederick Arthur, *Visitation of Ireland* (London, 1897–1918)

Hussey de Burgh, U. H., *The Landowners of Ireland. An alphabetical list of the owners of estates of 500 acres or £500 valuation and upwards in Ireland* (Dublin, 1881)

Joyce, P. W., *The Origin and History of Irish Place Names* (Dublin, 1913)

Knight of Glin & Griffin, D. J. & Robinson, N. K., *Vanishing Country Houses of Ireland* (Dublin, 1989)

Leet, Ambrose, *A Directory to the Market Towns, Villages, Gentlemen's Seats, and Other Noted Places in Ireland* (Dublin, 1814)

Leslie, Rev. James, *History of Kilsaran Union of Parishes in the County of Louth* (Dundalk, 1908)

Lewis, Samuel, *A Topographical Dictionary of Ireland* (London, 1837)

Lyons, Mary Cecelia, *Illustrated Incumbered Estates* (Whitegate, 1993)

Lyttleton, J. & O'Keeffe, T., *The Manor in Medieval and Early Modern Ireland* (Dublin, 2005)

MacDonnell, Randal, *The Lost Houses of Ireland* (London, 2002)

McGinley, Michael, *The La Touche Family in Ireland* (Greystones, 2004)

McGrath, Declan, *Scéal Gortleitreach, Lakefield* (Leitrim, 1991)

McParlan, James, *Statistical Survey of the County of Mayo* (Dublin, 1802)

Marsden, Simon, *In Ruins – The Once Great Houses of Ireland* (London, 1997)

O'Hanlon, Rev. J. C., O'Leary, Rev. E., *History of The Queen's County* (Dublin, 1914)

O'Toole, Jimmy, *The Carlow Gentry* (Carlow, 1994)

Rowe, David & Scallan, Eithne, *Houses of Wexford* (Whitegate, 2004)

Smith, Charles, *The Ancient and Present State of the County and City of Cork* (Dublin, 1750)

Taylor, Geoffrey, *The Emerald Isle* (London, 1952)

Weir, Hugh W. L., *Historical, Genealogical and Architectural Notes on Some Houses of Clare* (Whitegate, 1986)

Journals and Newspapers

Faulkner's Journal
Journal of the County Kildare Archaeological Society and Surrounding Districts
Journal of the Irish Georgian Society
Journal of the Kerry Archaeological and Historical Society
Journal of the Royal Society of Antiquaries Ireland
Leitrim Observer
Limerick Leader
Old Kilkenny Review
Ríocht na Midhe, Meath Archaeological and Historical Society
Shannonside Magazine
The Irish Builder
The Tuam Herald

Glossary

Civil War The Irish Civil War began on 28 June 1922 after the establishment of the Irish Free State. The war was fought between the forces of the Provisional Government, who supported the Anglo-Irish Treaty, and the Republican opposition, for whom the Treaty represented a betrayal of the Irish Republic. The Civil War ended on 24 May 1923 when Frank Aiken, IRA Chief of Staff, ordered the anti-treaty IRA volunteers to cease fighting and dump arms rather than surrender them to the Free State. The two main political parties, Fianna Fáil and Fine Gael, are the direct descendants of the opposing sides in the War.

Cromwell During the English Civil War (1641–1651), Oliver Cromwell served as one of the commanders on the Parliamentarian side which saw the Royalists defeated and King Charles I executed. Cromwell dominated the short-lived Commonwealth of England and ruled as Lord Protector from 1653 until he died from malaria in 1658.

In March 1649, the English Parliament commissioned Oliver Cromwell to lead an army of invasion into Ireland. Cromwell landed with his New Model Army at Dublin in August 1649 and started on the reconquest of Ireland. His subsequent brutal campaign resulted in the deaths of about 20 per cent of the Irish population. Cromwell confiscated large amounts of land. Land was often granted to Cromwell's soldiers of fortune in return for their services. The only major setback suffered by Cromwell was at Clonmel, where 2,000 English troops were killed in a failed attack. Cromwell left Ireland in May 1650, with his son-in-law, Henry Ireton, remaining as commander of the English forces. Most of Leinster, Munster and Ulster were in English hands by the end of 1650. Ireton died of fever in 1651, leaving Edmund Ludlow and Sir Charles Coote to accept the surrender of Galway in May 1652. After the restoration of the English monarchy in 1660, Charles II had Oliver Cromwell and Henry Ireton's corpses exhumed from Westminster Abbey. Their bodies were then hanged, drawn and quartered. Cromwell's body was thrown, minus its head, into a pit. This act of mutilation was carried out in retribution for signing the death warrant of Charles I. Cromwell's head remained in the possession of private collectors and museum owners until it was finally buried in March 1960.

Demesne Pronounced *domain*, originates from the Old French *demeine* and from the Latin *dominium*. When used in reference to a country house, the demesne is specifically the area of the land around the house retained by the owner for their own use and enjoyment. Normally the demesne would consist of gardens, lawns and other pleasure grounds.

Encumbered Estate Acts The Encumbered Estates Act of 1849 established the Encumbered Estates Court which was designed to handle the sale of insolvent land estates the owners of which had been bankrupted by the Great Famine. It was hoped that English investors would be attracted to buy Irish estates, thereby transforming

Irish agriculture. Contrary to the government's expectations, however, the vast majority of the purchasers were Irishmen from the established landed and professional elites.

On a creditor's petition, the court had the authority to enforce the sale of the estate. After the sale, the court distributed the money among the creditors and granted clear title to the new owners. The existing tenants were unprotected by the legislation and many new owners, particularly in the west of Ireland, used the opportunity of purchase to evict tenants.

In 1853 the functions of the Encumbered Estates Court were assumed by the Landed Estates Court. By 1859, over 5 million acres worth some £21 million had been sold by the courts.

The courts prepared a detailed account of the landed estates, including drawings, rents and records of tenants. These records have become a valuable resource for historians and genealogists.

Great Famine

In 1844 the potato blight *Phytophthora infestans* arrived in Ireland. In 1845 50 per cent of the potato crop was destroyed by the blight. Over 3 million people were totally dependent on potatoes for food and in 1846 when three-quarters of the crop was destroyed, the first deaths from starvation were recorded. From 1845 to 1852 the population of Ireland dropped by 25 per cent. Approximately 1 million people died from starvation and disease and a further 1 million emigrated.

Land Acts

From 1873 to 1896 Irish farmers suffered a depression in agricultural prices. Grain from America was cheaper and better, and meat could be sent in refrigerated ships from as far as New Zealand. Tenant farmers in Ireland were left with lower net incomes with which to pay their rent.

The Landlord & Tenant (Ireland) Act of 1870 was designed to increase the security of the tenant and also allow tenants to borrow the cost of buying their holding from the government, but had little effect.

The Land Law (Ireland) Act of 1881 gave the tenants real security through the creation of the Irish Land Commission which acted to fix and reduce rents.

The Purchase of Land (Ireland) Act of 1885, also known as the Ashbourne Act started the motion of tenant purchase.

The Land Purchase (Ireland) Act of 1903, also known as the Wyndham Act allowed for the advancing to tenants the sum necessary to purchase their holdings, repayable over a period of years on terms determined by an independent commission. The sale was not compulsory, but made attractive to both parties, based on the government paying the difference between the price offered by tenants and that demanded by landlords. After the introduction of the Wyndham Act, approximately 75 per cent of tenant farmers had bought out their landlords.

The Land Purchase (Ireland) Act of 1909 introduced compulsory purchase and after the Irish Free State was created in 1922 the government re-established the Land Commission which sought the compulsory purchase of untenanted estates so that they could be divided amongst farmers. The Land Commission continued to buy and distribute land until 1982 and was dissolved in 1999.

Plantations

During the sixteenth and seventeenth centuries, land which had been confiscated by the English government was colonised or planted with settlers from England and Scotland.

Property Tax and the removal of roofs

Prior to 1977 all domestic property in Ireland was taxed based on the 'rateable valuation' of the property. These 'rates' were collected by local authorities to provide for services such as mains water and refuse, etc. In some cases the roofs of large mansion houses were removed to avoid payment of rates.

MP/TD

In the Republic of Ireland, the term MP (Member of Parliament) refers either to members of the pre-1801 Parliament of Ireland or to Irish members elected to the House of Commons of the United Kingdom of Great Britain and Ireland from 1801 to 1922. Members of the current Republic of Ireland lower house of parliament, *Dáil Éireann*, are referred to as *Teachtaí Dála* or TDs. Members of the current Republic of Ireland upper house of parliament, *Seanad Éireann*, are referred to as *Seanadóirí* or Senators.

War of Independence

The Irish War of Independence was a guerrilla war mounted by the Irish Republican Army (IRA) against the British government and its forces in Ireland. The war began on 21 January 1919 following the declaration of independence by the revolutionary parliament of the Irish Republic at its first meeting in the Mansion House, Dublin, and continued until a truce was agreed in July 1921. The Anglo-Irish Treaty which was signed in London on 6 December 1921 saw the ending of British rule in most of Ireland and established the Irish Free State. Six northern counties remained within the United Kingdom as Northern Ireland.

Architectural terms

Bays	The number of windows in a horizontal line across a facade.
Bow	A curved wall or window.
Bracket	A projection from the face of a wall, the purpose of which is to support a structure or object.
Breakfront	A section that projects outwards from a building beyond the sections on each side.
Console	An ornamental scrolled bracket.
Corinthian	The most decorative style of ancient Greek buildings. The sides of Corinthian columns are fluted and their tops are decorated with scrolls, flowers and leaves.
Doric	The oldest and simplest of the ancient Greek building styles. Doric columns are of a plain, undecorated design.
Fanlight	Glazed area above a doorway, designed to brighten the hallway inside.
Ionic	A simply decorated style of ancient Greek buildings. Ionic columns are normally taller and more slender than Doric columns; the sides of the columns are fluted and the tops are decorated with scrolls.
Italianate	A style of architecture which is a romanticism of Italian architecture.
Moulding	The shaped profile given to any feature which projects from the face of a wall.
Mullion	An upright structural element dividing the glazed sections of a window.
Niche	A recess in a wall, usually for holding a statue or urn.
Oculus	A small circular panel or window.
Pediment	A triangular decorative structure at the top of a wall or over a doorway.
Portico	A porch or walkway with a roof supported by columns.
Quoin	The stone blocks on the outside corner of a building which are usually of a different material or decoration than the adjoining walls.

Acknowledgements

Thanks to: Brian Furey for research help on Kilsaran, James McCormick for research help on Doonass, Mark Thomas for research help on Rochestown and Kincraigie, Jessica Collins for photographs at the K Club and Lyons estate, Fiona Reilly for much proofreading, sketching and more proofreading, Margaret Reilly for proofreading, Alison Reilly for proofreading, Ger McCarthy for proofreading and his great knowledge of the Irish country house, Caroline Martin at Leitrim County Library for help on Drumhierny and Lakefield. Also thanks to Brian McCabe and Bella Walsh.